Praise for

The Suicide Solution

"We're in the middle of a second pandemic of depression. And as a pastor, I know from firsthand experience the damage left in the wake of suicide. What this book offers is a pathway out of the darkness and into the light—it's a peremptory strike against the dire threats of our broken biology and our broken narratives. And, even more important, the message and solutions offered in *The Suicide Solution* are embedded in, and drawn from, the Great Healer, who is Jesus. If you're struggling, or know someone who is, this book can be a lifesaver."

—**Dr. Derwin L. Gray,** founder and lead pastor of Transformation Church and author of *Building a Multiethnic Church*, *The Good Life*, and *Limitless Life*

"There has never been a more important time in history for *The Suicide Solution*. It is written with practical solutions that provide a new way forward for this epidemic problem. I highly recommend it."

—**Daniel Amen, M.D.,** founder and CEO of Amen Clinics and *New York Times* bestselling author of *The End of Mental Illness* and *Change Your Brain, Change Your Life*

"My heartbreak continues. Just as I was finishing *The Suicide Solution*, I learned of yet another teen suicide. It's hard to bear…*again*. Gratefully, in this important and hopeful work, Rick Lawrence and Dr. Daniel Emina provide a distinctly unique approach to this widespread and devastating societal problem. These authors shine a new light—a healing light, a much-needed Jesus light—into this epidemic. Lawrence and Emina gift us with medical tools, practical helps, and strong biblical undergirding as they teach us all how to be 'midwives of grace' to those in desperate places. We all need to read and reread this book."

—**Andrea Syverson,** founder of IER Partners, branding strategist, and author of *Alter Girl: Walking Away from Religion into the Heart of Faith*

"The balance of solid medical and psychological research with good theology and practical instruction makes this a unique and invaluable resource. Though the principles apply broadly to everyone interested in a whole and healthy life, the need for this type of help for those dealing with suicidal ideation and those trying to help them is immense. Thank you for speaking to this urgent need."

—**Pastor Todd Rodarmel,** lead pastor of Mountain View Church in San Juan Capistrano, California

"For those like me who care for those in despair, I can't think of a better gift. For those drowning while others seem to breathe easy, Daniel and Rick offer more than a lifeline—they offer shot after shot of hope."

—**Phil Callaway,** radio host and author of *Laugh Like a Kid Again*

"Dimensionally different from other integration efforts, this book does far more than offer Jesus's helpful perspective inside professionally defined challenges; readers travel through the wormhole of Christ's heart into the painful anguish of depression and suicide. When Jesus himself resets the parameters for discovery, what's most true casts light on what else is true. Marvelous assets from Amen Clinics and brain science breakthroughs become fish and loaves stretched to feed those hungry to hear from the Lord, making *The Suicide Solution* a feast of wonder, hope, and healing!"

—**Dr. Dave Rahn,** senior research advisor and former vice president of Youth for Christ USA and author of *Disrupting Teens with Joy*

"Rick Lawrence and Dr. Daniel Emina masterfully tackle a difficult and traumatic subject that continues to leave millions of people in unimaginable pain and suffering. This book offers hope through the lens of Jesus—a hope that is so desperately sought by people in the midst of the oft-times unspoken battle for their lives. Lawrence and Emina will get you thinking deeper as they explore the freedom promised to humanity in the gospels and delivered through Christ's sacrifice. *The Suicide Solution* is an absolute must-read."

—**Billy Hallowell,** director of communications and content for PureFlix.com, former senior editor at Faithwire.com, and author of *Playing with Fire*

"This is such a needed book in our cultural moment. If we only knew how many people struggled with this topic, not only would we be more empathic with others, but we would be more empathic with ourselves. I believe this book will bring healing and freedom to a lot of people. May it be, may it be!"

—**David Lomas,** pastor of Reality San Francisco and author of *The Truest Thing about You*

"The chasm separating the powerfully transformative gifts of a Christian spiritual life and the tools of therapeutic interventions has been too wide for too long, in effect leaving people to struggle with significant mental health issues alone. Rick Lawrence and Dr. Daniel Emina stand in that gap with this practical and carefully researched book. 'It's never just one thing'—that was one of the best things I learned from my own counseling degree program. And in a manner that is both groundbreaking and winsome, Lawrence and Emina tackle the cataclysm that is the meeting of nature, nurture, AND theological issues that causes disordered thinking and leads people to the drastic solution of taking their own lives. The ongoing epidemic of suicide has profound implications for Christians and Christian communities. This is a book that will help you love your friends and family more productively, and it will help ministry leaders come alongside the people that God has given to their care in deeper and more effective ways."

—**Dr. Nancy S. Going,** director of research and resource development for Vibrant Faith

The Suicide Solution

THE SUICIDE SOLUTION

Finding Your Way Out of the Darkness

Dr. Daniel Emina & Rick Lawrence

SALEM
BOOKS

an imprint of Regnery Publishing
Washington, D.C.

Unless otherwise marked, all scriptures marked are taken from the HOLY BIBLE, NEW LIVING TRANSLATION. Copyright © 1996, 2004, 2007 by Tyndale House Foundation. Used by permission of Tyndale House Publishers, Inc., Carol Stream, Illinois, 60188. All rights reserved.
Scriptures marked NASB are taken from the NEW AMERICAN STANDARD BIBLE®. Copyright © 1960, 1962, 1963, 1968, 1971, 1972, 1973, 1975, 1977, 1995 by the Lockman Foundation. Used by permission.
Scriptures marked TM are taken from THE MESSAGE: THE BIBLE IN CONTEMPORARY ENGLISH. Copyright © 1993, 1994, 1995, 1996, 2000, 2001, 2002. Used by permission of NavPress Publishing Group.

Salem Books™ is a trademark of Salem Communications Holding Corporation
Regnery® is a registered trademark and its colophon is a trademark of Salem Communications Holding Corporation

Cataloging-in-Publication data on file with the Library of Congress

ISBN: 978-1-68451-159-4
eISBN: 978-1-68451-205-8

Library of Congress Control Number: 2020952239

Published in the United States by
Salem Books
An Imprint of Regnery Publishing
A Division of Salem Media Group
Washington, D.C.
www.SalemBooks.com

Manufactured in the United States of America

10 9 8 7 6 5 4 3 2 1

Books are available in quantity for promotional or premium use. For information on discounts and terms, please visit our website: www.SalemBooks.com.

CONTENTS

FOREWORD

By Daniel G. Amen, M.D.

All my life, I've been surrounded by suicide.
    One of my aunts killed herself, as did my adopted son's biological father and my son-in-law's father. However, my first and most painful brush with suicide came in 1979 when, in my second year of medical school, someone I loved tried to take her own life. Fortunately, she survived the attempt, and I took her to see a wonderful psychiatrist for help. Over time, I realized that if he helped her (which he did), it would not only impact her, but also her children, loved ones, and even grandchildren—they would all be shaped by someone who was happier and more stable.

As a result of watching this transformation firsthand, I fell in love with psychiatry. I realized it had the potential to help generations of people. But the profession I'd grown to love was the only medical discipline that never looked at the organ it treats. I knew we could do better, especially when it came to suicide. The pain of suicide is unlike any other loss, because people see it as a choice to harm themselves, rather than as the outcome of an illness.

Brain imaging changes this stigmatizing belief.

Over the last thirty years, my colleagues and I at Amen Clinics have built the world's largest database of brain scans related to behavior. We've performed more than 170,000 brain SPECT (Single Photon Emission Computed Tomography) scans, which measure blood flow and activity patterns. Our brain-imaging work shows us that mental health is really brain health. When your brain works right, you work right. When your brain is troubled, for whatever reason, you tend to have trouble in your life. For people who are vulnerable to suicidal thoughts and behaviors, a troubled brain can have devastating consequences.

Brain-imaging studies performed at Amen Clinics on more than three hundred people who have attempted suicide reveal that certain brain patterns are common in those who take their own lives. Our research, which has been published in the peer-reviewed journals *Translational Psychiatry*,[1] *The Journal of Neuropsychiatry*, and *Clinical Neurosciences*,[2] shows that suicidality is associated with dysfunction in the brain's limbic system (emotional centers), impaired impulse control, and low cerebral blood flow (especially in the prefrontal cortex). SPECT studies also reveal that head injuries are associated with an increase in suicidality. For example, research shows that experiencing a single concussion triples the risk of suicide.[3]

It is clear that in order to have a healthy mind, you must first have a healthy brain. This has become more evident in the wake of the coronavirus pandemic as incidences of depression, anxiety, and suicide attempts have spiked.

In this timely book from Amen Clinics psychiatrist Daniel Emina, M.D., and award-winning author Rick Lawrence, you'll be introduced to the fascinating concept of the brain's biology as the "computer hardware" of your life and your brain's psychology (also encompassing your spiritual life) as its "computer software." The two work together to build a foundation for whole-person health—the "abundant life" Jesus promised to those who follow Him. They explore how "bugs" in our hardware and our human operating system can lead to negative thinking patterns, depression, and an increased vulnerability to suicide. More importantly, they reveal how optimizing your whole life— biological, psychological, social, and spiritual—is the key to eliminating those bugs and finding your way out of the "valley of the shadow of death."

INTRODUCTION

"**S**uicide is a permanent solution to a temporary problem." If you're wrestling with a life-or-death decision right now or know someone who is, you've probably heard this truth before. But can these words deliver the payload of rescue you (or your friend) so desperately need? We all know that words alone simply aren't enough. We need the right tools, not just the right words.

This book is a tool kit for people who need real help in their fight against the encroaching darkness. Using these tools, we've seen many people struggling with depression and suicidality come back from the brink. They get dramatically better.

We want you to know, at the moment you are reading these words, that you are not alone. *You are not alone.* Hope is real. Tangible. Possible. Together, guided by the "Good Shepherd," we'll find a way out of the "valley of the shadow of death" and emerge into the light again. Jesus said, "I came so that [you]

would have life, and have it abundantly" (John 10:10 NASB). And
He means what He says.

■ ■ ■

By the late 1980s, INXS was the top-selling band in the world,
dominating Billboard's Hot 100 with four top-ten singles and a
Grammy nomination for the album *Kick*. Fame and fortune rolled
over the band like a summer thunderstorm—and frontman Michael
Hutchence was its lightning rod. Mesmerized by what *Rolling Stone*
called Hutchence's "magnetic presence" on stage, fans crowned him
the spiritual successor to the Doors' Jim Morrison. But in 1997, alone
in a Ritz-Carlton hotel room in Sydney, Australia, the
thirty-seven-year-old former retail-store cashier died after asphyxiat-
ing himself with his own snakeskin belt. Though credible questions
about whether his death was the result of an autoerotic accident linger
to this day, the coroner's official report listed it as suicide.

The shock of his death obliterated one of the great rags-to-riches
stories in rock and roll history. And no one was more shaken by the
news than Hutchence's close friend Paul Hewson—a.k.a. Bono, leader
of the Irish rock band U2 and an outspoken follower of Jesus.

Bono had found in Hutchence a "bold and mischievous" spirit not
unlike his own—a man-child who understood the counterintuitive
loneliness of a rock icon. They were two working-class men—one from
Ireland, the other from Australia—who'd chased down an improbable
dream, then held on as it dragged them into the maelstrom of fame.
Failure is an obvious enemy, but a certain kind of success stalks like
an assassin.

Not long after the news of Hutchence's death broke, Bono channeled his grief into a song that later became a Grammy-winning single
on his band's 2000 album, *All That You Can't Leave Behind*. The
song is called "Stuck in a Moment You Can't Get Out Of," and it was

conceived as a fictional argument about suicide between Bono and his friend. "It's a row between mates," he explained. "You're kinda trying to wake them up out of an idea. In my case it's a row I didn't have while he was alive. I feel the biggest respect I could pay to him was not to write some stupid soppy song, so I wrote a really tough, nasty little number, slapping him around the head. And I'm sorry, but that's how it came out of me."

> *You've got stuck in a moment*
> *And now you can't get out of it*
> *Don't say that later will be better now*
> *You're stuck in a moment*
> *And you can't get out of it*

And then, perhaps, the words Bono would've spoken to his friend if he'd known how deep he'd descended into the darkness...

> *And if the night runs over*
> *And if the day won't last*
> *And if your way should falter*
> *Along the stony pass,*
> *It's just a moment*
> *This time will pass*[1]

"Stuck in a Moment" is a song about a friend who is sliding into a crevasse of despair, but it's also a song that captures our universal human experience—our rutted roundabouts of destructive thought patterns. We need a narrative of life, not death—or, in Bono's words: "You gotta stand up straight, carry your own weight...."

But how do we stand up straight when we don't have the strength to stand? And how do we carry our own weight when our shoulders are slumped and broken? And how do we stop those we care about from descending into a cave they might never find their way out of?

In June 2018, twelve boys from a soccer team and their coach ventured into a complex cave system in Thailand and got trapped after heavy rains drove them more than a mile deep into the inky dark. A massive rescue effort was launched, and divers discovered the emaciated teenagers ten days later. The monsoons were filling the cave system like a bathtub, and rescuers faced long odds to get them out in time. Meanwhile, oblivious to the full-throttle attempts to reach them, the boys battled to maintain hope as the days, hours, and minutes dragged by—how, they wondered, was rescue even possible? Death, like the water slowly creeping up the walls of their refuge, seemed inescapable.

For those who are right now waging a (mostly) secret war against anxiety, depression, and suicide, reality feels very much like that dark cave filling with water. It's just a matter of time, really, before death insinuates itself as a friend. This book is for those people and for anyone who cares for someone who's wandered into that cave and lost his or her way.

Rescue is possible. Help is on the way. Darkness will give way to light.

Patterns of Destructive Thinking

With college counseling centers facing an epidemic of students seeking help for emotional distress and with one-fifth of the adult population wrestling with depression, Western culture is facing a crisis affecting a wide swath of its population. The significant mental health consequences of the COVID-19 pandemic are wide-ranging, impacting an entire generation as profoundly as 9/11 did. We've seen an increase in loneliness, anxiety, depression, post-traumatic stress disorder (PTSD), substance use disorder—and a broad range of other mental and behavioral disorders, including domestic violence and child abuse. At the height of the pandemic, one-quarter of all eighteen- to twenty-four-year-olds said they'd "seriously considered" suicide in the last month.[2] This wave of emotional distress has prompted a spike in mental health diagnoses and the meteoric growth of the self-help industry. Unfortunately, the common solutions offered to those beset by anxiety, depression, and "suicidality" are often shallow—they lack both efficacy and real hope, and they perpetuate an internal focus that isolates and builds on false narratives.

The common thread among those who are scrambling to avoid slipping even deeper into suicidal ideation (perpetual thoughts about planning your own death) is their inability to overcome stuck patterns of destructive thinking. Conventional approaches to dealing with this crisis often have a "surface" feel—pay attention to your mood swings and behavioral changes, then seek counseling or pharmaceuticals when you see warning signs. These are reactive—not proactive—strategies. We need ways to respond to this crisis that focus on its roots, not just its fruits. "Destructive narratives" that become embedded in our internal "story" keep us stuck in this slow-moving avalanche of hopelessness.

A computer's hardware is made up of the tangible and physical components that are necessary for storing and running software. Hardware serves as a delivery system for the set of instructions, or "code," that the software provides. Software is intangible—a collection of programs or instructions that enables users to interact with the hardware to accomplish specific tasks. Both work to determine the functional capabilities of a computer system.

In human beings, our "hardware" is our biology (specifically, our brain), and our "software" is our thought process or psychology. Together, they guide how we experience and interact with our world in predictable and adaptive ways. And together, our hardware/software identity forms our experiences, capabilities, limitations, susceptibilities, and possibilities. Suicide is generally the culmination of a malfunction or failure of the brain's hardware (biology) and software (psychology), which are hardwired to support self-preservation. This is the result of a "multi-system failure" that coincides with what seems to be insurmountable stressors.

Another way to understand the human operating system (software) is to think of it as our "story." Story works to construct, give meaning to, and set boundaries around our experience of reality. Our story is the "narrative code" that unlocks the meaning behind our experiences in life. The story we tell ourselves about ourselves determines how we function and influences our limitations and possibilities in life. Dan McAdams, a professor of psychology at Northwestern University, calls this our "narrative identity"—it's our own personal mythology, complete with plot twists, thematic threads, and heroes and villains. McAdams says we tell ourselves two basic self-narratives: 1) Redemptive Stories, and 2) Contamination Stories. The first kind of story is transplanted from the Kingdom of God, where redemption is not only the mission of the Messiah, but also the heartbeat of life. The second kind of story is exported and propagated by the Kingdom of Darkness, where "killing, stealing, and destroying" (John 10:10) is the mission.

The "bugs" (or viruses) in our story are destructive narratives that operate, often undetected, in the background of our emotional/spiritual/psychological operating system—distortions that cause us to perceive reality, and our own story, inaccurately. Vulnerabilities to these bugs are sometimes predetermined by our "hardware"—the biology we inherit through genetics or that is written into our code by our experiences, upbringing, or choices (which introduce viruses or buggy software). When bugs go undetected or unchallenged, they grow into contamination stories, sometimes so subtly that we can no longer separate our true identity from the corrupted version the contaminants have produced. Some of us never overcome our bugs—and when that happens, we are susceptible to recurrent bouts with mental illness, or we can inadvertently infect others with our way of thinking. Many of us—really most of us, according to the National Institutes of Health[3]—go through seasons when we are stuck so deeply in our ruts that the walls closing in on us make it seem as though we are at the bottom of the Grand Canyon.

Out of the Valley of the Shadow of Death

We become the story we've decided to live inside (or have been cornered into). When Jesus launched His public ministry by proclaiming, "I have come to set captives free" (Luke 4:18), He meant that He'd come to tell us the truth about our story and to "debug" us. You could say that Jesus's de-captivating mission is to offer tech support for our human hardware/software issues—to find the destructive narratives embedded in our story and eradicate them. But He will not do this unilaterally in our life; in the Kingdom of God, transformation is always tied to invitation. Jesus is inviting us to partner with Him to first surface, then move past our debilitating bugs. This means the way out of the "valley of the shadow of death" is a hike led by a trusted Guide, not a click-your-heels-and-return-to-Kansas solution. We follow the Guide because we've decided to invest our trust in Him, based on our knowledge of who He is and our experience with His heart. Along the path out of the valley, there are mileposts:

1. Understand the multiple contributors to how we feel and behave. Our genetics, life experiences, unique temperaments and personalities, brain injuries, chronic health challenges, infections, and toxin exposures are stacked stressors that generate brain illness. Hardware that is compromised, and software that is corrupted, have an inexorable dragging impact.

2. Know who you are—your strengths, goals, and passions. Our giftings come pre-packaged with vulnerabilities (for example, analytical, empathetic, and creative people all have distinct "soft spots" that come into play when the person is exposed to trauma or repeated life stressors that can't be controlled, explained, or resolved). Our vulnerabilities are charged with emotional impact. They can be further complicated by a lack of quality community connections or an unhealthy interior narrative.

3. Maintain your hardware and software, using routine debugging or "virus protection" practices. This means living a lifestyle that continually refreshes your story, maintains an open invitation to the "co-authoring" presence of Jesus, nurtures a healthy thought life that matches your values, and pursues a healthy nutritional and exercise lifestyle. Maintenance also involves nurturing your creativity, your healthy relational connections, contributing to your community, and having an intentional approach to life.

Freedom from Captivity

The way out of our "valley of the shadow of death" is through Jesus. "I am the way, the truth, and the life" is much more than an inspirational promise; it's the passionate determination of a Shepherd who leaves the "ninety-nine" protected sheep grazing on the hillside to find and free the "one" sheep that has wandered away into the brambles that hold him captive (John 14:6 and Matthew 18:12–14).

And those who are struggling with anxiety, depression, and suicide are all the one sheep.

Sheep caught in the brambles are desperate to free themselves from the captive power of their bugged computer system and their stacked stressors. But none of us has to stay broken. We don't have to descend a mile deep into our brokenness in the first place. And we don't have to watch from the cave's entrance while the people we love slip from our grasp and disappear deeper into the darkness.

In this book, we will embrace Jesus's strategies for intervening in the downward cycles of despair in ourselves and others and discover that His paths into freedom are (not surprisingly) supported and spotlighted by the emerging "best practices" of the scientific and psychiatric communities.

This book is the fruit of an ongoing conversation between a theologian/ministry practitioner and a psychiatric therapist/researcher. Along the way, we'll fold in the voices of those who are struggling to find their way out of "the valley of the shadow of death" and have discovered the guiding hand of Jesus pulling them to safety. Drawing from the transformational "whole person" strategies of Jesus and informed by a deep perspective on the clinical realities of anxiety, depression, and suicide, we will chart a path into life and freedom. The goal is to help ourselves and others embrace a narrative of life instead of death.

IT'S A HARDWARE/ SOFTWARE PROBLEM

E very fourteen minutes, someone dies by suicide in the United States. It's the tenth leading cause of death overall and the second leading cause of death for those ten to thirty-four years of age.[1] Soon, if this nasty trajectory perpetuates, suicide will eclipse "unintentional injury" as the #1 killer of teenagers. Since 1999, suicide has increased by 33 percent, decreasing our overall life expectancy, while deaths from cancer during the same period have dropped by 27 percent.[2] More broadly, average life expectancy in the U.S. has declined for three straight years—fed by a higher death rate among "working-age" Americans between twenty-five and sixty-four, whose deaths are linked primarily to drug overdoses, suicides, and alcohol-related diseases. The United States is the only wealthy country in the world that is experiencing this trend.[3]

Half of all Americans will struggle with a mental health issue at some point in their lives, according to a large epidemiological study. Anxiety disorders (28 percent), depression (21 percent), impulse control disorders (25 percent), and substance use disorders (15 percent)

1

are the most common. Half of all these conditions start by age four-teen, and 75 percent start by age twenty-four.[4]

I (Daniel) have worked at the Amen Clinics for close to a decade. During this intense season of research and practice, the boundaries of my training in psychiatry have expanded far beyond what I learned in my years as a general psychiatry resident and during my child and adolescent psychiatry fellowship. At the Amen Clinics, we approach treatment with a foundational belief that each person is born with a purpose. We see brain health as a vital part of achieving this purpose. We believe that if your brain works right, you work right. We leverage our lessons from neuroimaging (SPECT scans), combined with a functional medicine approach, to shift the focus from "mental health issues" to "brain health issues." This shift has been transformative. It reframes our approach to treating serious psychological dysfunctions, including suicide, from the perspective of "fault-based" to "medical condition–based." If suicidal ideation is predictable and treatable, then we can intervene to prevent its consequences the same way we intervene in the processes that lead to high blood pressure, diabetes, or obesity. In other words, we can "flatten the curve" of the suicidality epidemic.

In the Old Testament, the people of God constructed a Temple to house the presence of God; we who live under the "New Covenant" offer our own bodies as "the temple of the Holy Spirit." Paul reminds us: "Don't you realize that your body is the temple of the Holy Spirit, who lives in you and was given to you by God?" (1 Corinthians 6:19). We are caretakers of the New Temple, and the stability of our "housing" is determined by our hardware and software. Corruption in either one, resulting in brain illness, compromises the foundation of the house. And God wants the house that He lives in to stand in the face of struggle and disappointment and trauma: "Though the rain comes in torrents and the floodwaters rise and the winds beat against that house, it won't collapse because it is built on bedrock" (Matthew 7:25).

I (Rick) have been studying, teaching, and living by the practices and priorities of Jesus for decades. I'm the general editor of *Jesus-Centered Bible*, host of the podcast *Paying Ridiculous Attention to Jesus*, and the author of more than thirty books and curricula, all focusing on the "most-known, least-known" person in human history. In 2013, *Time* magazine's editors named Jesus "the most significant person in history." He is Messiah to millions and "great teacher" or "spiritual leader" to millions more. But Jesus would describe Himself differently. His mission on Earth, of course, was to sacrifice His Son-of-God life to pay the price for our sin and build a bridge back to make it possible for us to have an intimate relationship with God. But more broadly, He came to restore our fundamental humanity—our created-in-the-image-of-God wholeness.

At the beginning of His ministry, He gathered a large crowd on the side of a hill in Galilee and painted for them an epic canvas of what a full, healthy life actually looked like. "The Beatitudes," the prelude to what we now call "The Sermon on the Mount" (Matthew 5 and 6), is a series of eight broad blessings, all beginning with "Blessed are those who..." But these "blessings" are actually carefully chosen markers for building and maintaining a healthy, stable temple of the Holy Spirit. Over the next two chapters, He switched from a wide-angle to a telephoto lens—pinpointing what health looks like in relationships, self-care, finances, self-esteem, and spiritual maturity. To close out this thundering, poetic invitation into the "abundant life," Jesus revealed what sort of fruit a life infected by the "standards and practices" of His home culture, the Kingdom of God, produces:

> That is why I tell you not to worry about everyday life—whether you have enough food and drink, or enough clothes to wear. Isn't life more than food, and your body more than clothing? Look at the birds. They don't plant or harvest or store food in barns, for your heavenly Father

feeds them. And aren't you far more valuable to him than they are? Can all your worries add a single moment to your life? And why worry about your clothing? Look at the lilies of the field and how they grow. They don't work or make their clothing, yet Solomon in all his glory was not dressed as beautifully as they are. And if God cares so wonderfully for wildflowers that are here today and thrown into the fire tomorrow, he will certainly care for you. Why do you have so little faith?

So don't worry about these things, saying, "What will we eat? What will we drink? What will we wear?" These things dominate the thoughts of unbelievers, but your heavenly Father already knows all your needs. Seek the Kingdom of God above all else, and live righteously, and he will give you everything you need. (Matthew 6:25–33)

A healthy temple, then, is characterized by trust, not anxiety. A pervading sense of well-being in the face of need. A determination to hope that "leavens" circumstantial darkness. And peace, peace, peace of … mind.

Jesus invites us to love Him with "all [our] heart, soul, mind, and strength" (Mark 12:30)—and "all" translates to hardware and software restored into wholeness. Healthy brains beget healthy minds. And a healthy brain—like a healthy body or healthy spiritual life or healthy psychology—is the product of a fitness mentality. The function of our brain is not fixed; it constantly changes in the context of biological influences, psychological influences, social influences, and spiritual influences.

Depression, anxiety, and suicide can be related to our traumas, our learned way of thinking, or our genetic risks. And at Amen Clinics, we've discovered other contributors—head injuries, exposure to mold or environmental toxins, severe gut-health issues, and even infectious diseases such as Lyme or toxoplasmosis. These factors compromise the function of a brain, leading to symptoms like depression, anxiety, memory problems, focus problems, and suicidality.

It only makes sense that the One who created our biology and our psychology is the most qualified to offer us tech support when bugs infect our brain. Redemption is broader and deeper than a ticket to Heaven; Jesus intends to first surface what has caused us to be stuck in patterns of self-destruction, then restore our operating system to wholeness.

We begin by focusing on how our hardware and software work together to create healthy wholeness and what happens when something goes awry with either—or both.

CHAPTER 1

AN ESSENTIAL GUIDE TO THE STUCK BRAIN

What We Know about the Biological and Psychological Triggers for Suicide and Why Some Are More Vulnerable to Them Than Others

Imagine your brain is a car making its way down a rutted dirt road after a heavy rain. Your tires bounce in and out of potholes and slide side-to-side on the muddy route. It's a rough ride; sometimes your steering wheel has a mind of its own. Let's say the potholes represent the expected ups and downs we all experience on life's messy roads—disappointments, painful experiences, stress, loneliness, and even trauma.

Driving that car through the muddy ruts is challenging. You're trying to avoid the worst of the hazards and keep the momentum going as your suspension takes a beating. And then, just ahead, you see a wide rut filled with water—so you slow down to avoid damaging your car as you drive into it. But the hole is so deep that your car high-centers and your tires lose traction. It feels like a chasm, not a rut. You "gun" your engine in an attempt to vault out of it, but the squealing tires quickly dig a deeper hole. The harder you try, the deeper you sink. You try to reverse out of the hole, but that doesn't work either. Soon you are hopelessly stuck. With no way out and no one who can (or will) help, you consider abandoning your car altogether.

This is what it's like to "drive" a brain that finds itself stuck in a psychological pothole. It's a desperate feeling—frustrating and frightening and (eventually) hopeless. However, if we understand better how our car (or brain) gets stuck in the first place, we can learn how to avoid or navigate the deeper potholes on our rutted roads and keep moving through life's obstacles toward our destination. And even when we do get stuck, we can learn how to move past hopelessness to embrace strategies that will help us get unstuck. But before we explore the mechanics of a stuck brain, three stories will help us to put "skin" on the dangers facing those who know firsthand what happens when your car can't make it out of a pothole.

Julia's* Story

For years, my (Rick's) wife and I traveled a pitted road with a close friend (let's call her Julia) whose husband was psychologically abusive and controlling. As she grew to trust us, and as she came to know Jesus more deeply through our relationship, Julia shared more details about her reality and pleaded with us for advice. We were, of course, alarmed by her situation, but we knew she'd have to choose her own way out of it—we could not decide for her. We told her the truth: that she was living in an abusive situation that was not likely to get better, but we couldn't determine when "too much was too much." So for a long time, she wavered between making the best of a horrible situation and getting out altogether. Finally, one day while her husband was at work, she franticly packed her things and readied her young daughter to move into a friend's basement apartment. After a month there, we found her a house-sitting arrangement that guaranteed her safety for another six months.

At first, Julia seemed to be moving toward independence in her life—she started a job search, kept up her devotional reading and Bible

---

* Names marked with an asterisk (*) are pseudonyms.

study, and tried to recover from years of tension and fear. But slowly, our contact with her inexplicably decreased—she became distant and "fuzzy" in her interactions with us. At the end of those six months, she made the decision to move back into her home with her husband, telling us only after she was back with him again. And then, a few weeks later, she showed up on our doorstep with an armload of her journals and other personal papers. She said she wanted us to have them so that others would know "the true me" after she was gone. It was time to intervene:

"Julia, are you thinking of ending your life?" I asked.

Her eyes filled with tears and she gave me a slight nod.

"Do you have a plan you've worked out?"

Again, a slight nod.

"Can you please tell me your plan?"

In a soft, matter-of-fact voice, she described her strategy and timeline. I told her we needed to get her some help, right then. She looked perplexed, as if in a trance. I told her we'd like to take her to a hospital emergency room for her own safety. She nodded in agreement. I asked if I could have her phone, and she gave it to me. That seemed to startle her awake:

"I have to call my husband and tell him," she said.

I gently deferred: "How about you call him after we have you checked in at the hospital?"

We knew that if she called him first, he would prevent her from getting the help she needed. He was a violent man with a short fuse.

So we took Julia to the hospital, got her checked in, and then I gave her phone back (her husband had been trying to contact her the whole time). She called right away, explained where she was, and got off the phone. By the time he came rushing into the ER waiting room, she had already been admitted. The hospital staff understood the situation, and they told her husband he could not visit her yet. So he sat across the waiting room and glared at us, seething over our "betrayal."

For the next few months, our friend was treated first in a hospital setting and then in an outpatient facility. We tried to visit, but her husband threatened us with violence, and the tension he generated was so thick that Julia grew to dread our check-ins. Eventually, we lost all contact. From the snippets we've heard from others who know her, she now lives like a captive in her own home, occasionally venturing out for "work release." Over the years, we've seen her out in public two or three times. Once, when she was not with her husband, she reached out to embrace my wife and daughter with tears in her eyes, hesitantly grateful to reconnect. But after a few awkward moments, she retreated back inside her vacant shell. Perhaps she has now made peace with the hell she lives in; perhaps the experience has diminished her husband's abusive behavior. Or maybe she murdered her soul so the rest of her could survive. In the season of our close friendship, we helped to push and pull her car out of the deep rut she'd fallen into, but once she was free, the "pull of the rut" was too strong, and she shifted into reverse, backing into her familiar "stuckness."

Julia has lost her way—"confused and helpless, like [a] sheep without a shepherd" (Matthew 9:36). But Jesus understands the psychology of stuckness ("If the light you think you have is actually darkness, how deep that darkness is!" Matthew 6:23), and He is determined to invite those who are captive to it into freedom.

Zane's* Story

My (Daniel's) friend Zane is a social worker and a counseling patient who knows "how deep the darkness" can get. His journey out of captivity into freedom has been long and frightful. In his own words, this is what it feels like to follow Jesus out of the valley of the shadow of death.

As someone who dealt with intermittent suicidal ideations
for roughly twenty years, one of the most powerful words

for me has been "survivor." There were days I had to tell myself: *If I get through the day and don't take my life then that is a victory. If I don't go buy that gun, if I don't use that knife, if I don't jerk that steering wheel into oncoming traffic, if I don't hang myself, if I don't put that hose in my car's tailpipe, if I don't go into the garage and start the car, if I don't jump off that cliff or overpass, if I don't swallow all those pills, then that is a victory.*

I was determined to make it out: I am a survivor and I am going to one day tell people how I survived and what I survived. The idea that this suffering was "not for naught" helped me. I became a student of suffering. I studied and read a lot about it. I hoped to eventually use this season of suffering to try to help others. I wanted to become a "wounded healer." It was a reason to not punch out.

Because of my mental health struggles, I could do more than sympathize with those who suffer; I could empathize. I could sit beside a struggling person and say, "I get it—I've been where you are and felt what you feel." I could offer the "ministry of presence," not only "the ministry of proc-lamation." My pen and my pad (journal) and my phone were my weapons. I wrote out many prayers. I called and texted friends, raising my hand for help—a difficult word for many men to utter. I used coded language ("I'm bat-tling") to invite others to help with my self-harming thoughts. Telling someone "I am suicidal" was too hard—too shameful. But admitting "I'm battling" or "I'm dealing with hurtful thoughts" was easier to say.

I thought of myself as an Overcomer, and that was incredibly empowering for me. It was a reminder that I could (and will) win this war. Battle-quotes from the film *Dunkirk* resonated with me: "Survival is victory" and

"Hope is a weapon." And I used Scripture to fight back. I memorized a lot of it, repeating verses over and over to help counter the bombardment of harmful images that flashed in my mind. Scenes of death often plagued me. Sometimes my Scripture strategy helped, other times it didn't ward off the despair.

I committed certain scriptures to memory that I thought would help me tell my story to others. I believed that the specific way I was afflicted would be the specific way I would be able help folks—my niche. My brand of suffering was tailor-made for me, so I could enter into others' tailor-made realities. And that hope helped me endure.

My parents were lifelines, but sometimes I didn't want to describe the depths of my suicidal ideations, so I would only share these nightmares with my therapist. Talk therapy was extremely helpful. It was so key for me to bring harmful thoughts from the darkness into the light. I journeyed with one psychologist for more than ten years. In my last session with him, I gave him a single match from a book of matches and shook his hand, vowing to never extinguish my flame. It was a symbolic gesture. I wanted that transaction ingrained in my memory. I didn't want to ever break that promise.

I didn't always suffer well. It was ugly, and I've left a lot of carnage in my path. The illness often shut me down. But I often prayed, "Jesus, help me—take what I've been through and use it for others." Medication has helped alleviate the suicidal ideations substantially. Now, when I have suicidal thoughts, I'm able to dismiss them quickly. Meanwhile, I've lost clients, two uncles, and a mentor to suicide. I have felt the sting of death from the inside and the outside.

And, by God's grace channeled through the help of others, I am a Survivor....

Simon Peter's Story

His friend and rabbi Jesus has been arrested and "escorted" in the dead of night to the high priest Caiaphas's home, where the Jewish religious leaders have coerced a herd of false witnesses to offer up "proof" that He is deserving of death. In the courtyard, by the fire, Simon Peter is warming his hands and waiting to see how it all will end. Already he is wrestling over the implications of the passionate promises he has made to Jesus: "Even if everyone else deserts you, I never will" (Mark 14:29) and "Heaven forbid, Lord—this will never happen to you!" (Matthew 16:22). Inside the high priest's home, where the ridiculous assertions of His accusers have all been exposed, two eyewitnesses finally report something Jesus actually said: "This man said, 'I am able to destroy the Temple of God and rebuild it in three days.'" The high priest demands to know if Jesus claims to be the Messiah, finally dragging an answer out of the silent man in front of him: "You have said it." And then they beat him and mock him, the noise of the assault loud enough for Peter to hear.

And now, his eyes furtive and darting, Peter is defensive when a few bystanders accuse him of being a disciple: "Woman, I do not know him!" (Luke 22:57). His pathetic denials crescendo into a ludicrous proclamation: "Man, I don't know what you're talking about!" (verse 60). And the cock crows. And Jesus turns to look him in the eye. And Peter disintegrates into tears and disappears into the darkness.

He's not there along the Via Dolorosa to see Jesus drag His cross toward Golgotha. He's not there when the spikes are nailed into His hands or the spear is shoved into His side or the veil of the temple is torn in two. He's not there when Jesus's body is carried into a rich man's tomb, and he's not there to help roll a massive stone across its entrance. He's not there, when he's always been there. But maybe, wherever he's holed up, he feels the shake of the earthquake when Jesus takes His last breath—the rending of the earth that trumpets a new Earth and a new Heaven. Peter is like a man buried alive in a mine.

What is happening there in Peter's "dark night of the soul," when he is over-burdened by the crushing weight of his repeated denials? With his identity in shambles and on the heels of his shameful public cowardice, he has lost himself. What is he to hope for now? He can't go forward, and he can't go back. He is stuck. Maybe, like his former friend Judas the betrayer, it is time to end it all.

The loss of your identity is the worst thing that can happen to a person—worse than death, if that kind of "worse" can be imagined. People beset by suicidal ideation know this truth very well—when death insinuates itself as welcome relief in the face of the obliterating loss of self. Simon Peter, the over-confident alpha male who was the first to name Jesus "the Christ" and always the first to defend Him, is now exposed as a poser; he has now become a living metaphor for Jesus's blunt warning: "But the one who has heard and has not acted accordingly, is like a man who built a house on the ground without any foundation; and the torrent burst against it and immediately it collapsed, and the ruin of that house was great" (Luke 6:49). But we know this "dead man walking" somehow creeps back out of his hole after the resurrection of Jesus and faces up to his darkness by exposing himself to the Light. There, on the beach of the Sea of Galilee, Jesus drags his shame to the surface by asking three times: "Do you love me?"

Judas's sorrow and shame differ from Peter's in at least one crucial respect: Judas believes that his true identity is "betrayer, a poser, a nothing." Suicide is not such a radical decision when you've already determined that the you you've always seen yourself to be is now a nothing, a vapor that only hints at the person who was once a solid. The story of Judas is heartbreaking and distinct in comparison to

Peter's refusal to take his own life and his choice instead to move toward Jesus for help to escape the pothole that has captured him.

Why Are Some More Vulnerable to Suicide?

Like more than sixteen million adults in the U.S. today,[1] Julia, Zane, and Simon Peter have wrestled with the impact of a major depressive episode in their lives. For many, that "episode" is really more like their new normal. Suicidal ideation is embedded in their emotional weather patterns, lingering like a winter storm on the horizon. And the number of people worldwide who succumb to this darkness is staggering—more than one million end their own lives every year, according to the World Health Organization.[2] Down through history, that cascading number includes many well-known cultural influencers, from Marc Antony (Roman general and politician) to Anthony Bourdain (host of *Parts Unknown*) to Fidel Castro Díaz-Balart (son of Fidel Castro) to Kurt Cobain (lead singer/songwriter for Nirvana) to George Eastman (inventor and philanthropist) to Margot Kidder (actress who played Lois Lane in *Superman*) to Richard Manuel (lead singer of The Band) to Freddie Prinze (actor and star of *Chico and the Man*) to Anne Sexton (poet) to Kate Spade (fashion designer) to Alan Turing (mathematician and World War II codebreaker) to Vincent van Gogh (artist) to Robin Williams (actor and stand-up comedian). It's an endless, heartbreaking funeral procession.

So why do some of us remain stuck while others seem to bounce through the potholes and keep on going in life? What makes some people more vulnerable to the pull of suicide than others? In the famous first line of his classic novel *Anna Karenina*, Leo Tolstoy writes: "Happy families are all alike; every unhappy family is unhappy in its own way."[3] Translated into this context, every healthy brain is alike in its "wholeness," but every stuck brain is stuck in its own way. These are the factors that catalyze a descent into the darkness:

1. The brain's "self-preservation" mechanisms experience a breakdown.

Our brains are hardwired to help us survive. When internal and external stressors overwhelm these "fail-safe" mechanisms, our natural protections stop working properly. The anxiety we experience in the course of everyday life is deeply linked to our fundamental determination to preserve ourselves. Anxiety is a normal emotion; it's the brain's alarm system, letting us know when something is wrong so we can start the process of fixing the problem. But when our response to the alarm is dysfunctional, or our alarm system itself doesn't work the way it's designed to work, our self-preservation safeguards fail us.

Let's say our car alarm goes off. We rush outside, fumbling with our keys. Maybe there's a real threat to contend with. Or maybe the alarm system is over-sensitive and got activated when another car drove past a little too closely. Or maybe it was really the neighbor's car alarm, not our own. The first thing we do is assess if there's a real threat to our car; if we determine there is, we do something to mitigate the threat. When our alarm system is working correctly, anxiety alerts us to a danger, we locate the source of that sensation, then we take action to preserve our safety. When something's wrong with the system or we repeatedly overreact or underreact to the alarm, we dig ourselves into an anxiety rut that gets deeper as our deregulated threat response spins its wheels.

This alarm-response mechanism is hardwired into our caveman/woman "mainframe." When our cave-dweller ancestors emerged into the sunlight every morning, they saw a beautiful environment that also could be hiding a saber-toothed tiger. To survive, they had to assess potential threats properly—to "see past the bushes," so to speak. If they saw paw prints on the ground, that rustling in the bushes took on new meaning. If they responded poorly to the threat-clues around them, and did it often, their survival was at risk. I see the paw prints and the bushes rustling—what do I do with that? How do I decode the anxious feeling inside me? If we know what to do, then we thank our brain's anxiety response for the heads-up. But if we don't know what to do with it, or if we have an intolerance for anxious feelings, or if we haven't been taught how to properly gauge the risks raised by our anxiety response, the system that was designed to help us actually hurts us.

Some are "born" with a faulty alarm system where genetics, direct trauma, or trauma within the family have altered the "factory specs." Trauma is a powerful teacher: Remember that time you almost got eaten by a tiger? Every rustling bush is hiding a tiger! A brain that has experienced trauma or has been raised in a traumatic environment has had its assessment strategies hindered. Other health factors play into this as well—for example, immune-related disorders that produce inflammation in the body can have an impact on our alarm system that is similar to trauma. Our inherent threat-assessment skills are tied to our cognitive functioning. We can be taught how to manage our stressors better (fix our software), but we'll also need to address the biological problems (the hardware issues) that are hampering our ability to learn.

2. **Bugs in the brain's software (or our psychology) create "cognitive distortions" that lead to hopelessness, negative self-evaluations, and dire predictions for the future.**

These cognitive distortions undermine our social behavioral skills and:

- Radically diminish our problem-solving ability
- Tempt us to avoid solving problems in the first place
- Keep us stuck in existing ways of thinking ("cognitive rigidity")
- Limit our "menu" of healthy coping mechanisms

Software bugs also tamp down our "resilience traits"; those include a positive self-concept, optimistic attitude, and grateful mindset. With our emotional grit under fire, life's negative stressors seem like a heavyweight fighter pounding an opponent who's up against the ropes. Our sense of value, self-worth, safety, meaning, hope, and connectedness feels pummeled. We make rash decisions that blow past our self-regulators. A youth pastor friend sent an email to me (Rick) after one of his "regular" students took his own life, writing, "He's been at [our church] since preschool. He's volunteered in our kids' ministry and in missions. He never missed a small group—an overall great guy with a serious life plan who just let the emotion of a moment overtake him. So heartbreaking."

Because our brain hates dissonance, we are apt to create false narratives to help explain the pummeling we're experiencing. So the effect of cognitive distortion when we're battling stress is to magnify and multiply the challenge. Writing in *Europe's Journal of Psychology*, three psychology professors at the University of Western Ontario pinpoint this magnifying dynamic: "A lack of adequate problem-solving and a tendency to engage in problem-solving avoidance contribute to hopelessness and to negative evaluations about self and future, both of which are associated with greater suicide ideation. Because the individual avoids solving problems or has difficulty solving them, his or her stressors may be exacerbated, and he or she may therefore feel unable to improve his or her situation, leading to hopelessness and negative thoughts about self and future."[4] Stuckness is typified by a looping pattern of self-fulfilling prophecies that exists to serve and promote our false narratives.

To cope, some who are dealing with a stuck brain try to reverse their way out of the rut by self-medicating. But substance abuse further hinders problem-solving and is itself an avoidance strategy. It's a false and ineffective traction-substitute. And, improbably, some people use suicidal ideation as a coping strategy to deal with the bugs in their software. I (Daniel) used to have a professor who would deal with his anxiety and stress by obsessively planning his vacation; over-investing in a future free of stress was his coping strategy. In a similar way, some people use thoughts of death (a future release from the stress of life) as their coping strategy; they play with suicide scenarios often as an alternate form of emotional "self-medication."

3. **Bugs in the brain's hardware (or biology) create "broken links" in the areas tasked with managing our emotions and impulse regulation.**

A team of psychiatrists set out to identify "brain alterations that contribute to suicidal thoughts and behaviors," poring over the data from more than a hundred imaging studies over the course of two decades. They published their findings in the journal *Molecular Psychiatry*. They discovered a pattern of broken links in the brains of suicidal patients—a "dysregulation" of the specific brain regions and circuits that are supposed to maintain a stable emotional response to stressors.[5]

The prefrontal cortex (PFC), in particular, has a well-established role in self-reflection—an important governor on the false narratives that feed on our stressors. The PFC regulates both positive and negative internally generated emotions, orders the facts of past and imagined future events into a cohesive narrative, and determines how we respond to positive feedback (called "reward processing"). Healthy-functioning hardware (the PFC and limbic brain) helps us assess the relative threat of a stressor, then come up with a plan to cope with that stressor and switch to another strategy if the first one doesn't seem to be working. In other words, debugged hardware gives us flexibility and "agency" as we confront hard things in our life. We don't "camp" on negative thoughts or narratives. Instead, we challenge attacks on our self-image, and we fuel positive responses to challenges—optimism, motivation, and hopefulness. When our hardware is bug-free, even compromised software has a hard time affecting our ability to function long-term in a healthy way. And healthy hardware helps us learn new ways of thinking and coping.

If your computer is overheating, "bugged" software may be demanding too many system resources, forcing the CPU to work harder than it needs to. Or the source might, instead, be a broken fan (hardware) that is supposed to be cooling the system. If the fan is broken, better software may help, but the system will still run below its capability. The best way to solve the problem is to address both the software and hardware issues that are contributing to overheating.

Contrary to our assumptions, our brain's hardware is not static—it can be damaged or altered by several factors, including:

- **Genetic variants.** Our baseline ability to regulate serotonin or stress hormones like cortisol can impact our innate stress response. Our neurochemical makeup—the neurotransmitters and hormones (testosterone, estrogen, cortisol, for example)—and the neurons they act on are the "highway system" of our brain. Neurotransmitters are like messengers—each one delivers dispatches that prompt different cell functions. It's the way the brain talks to itself. The communication paths (or roads) are like circuits. Along the path the messengers knock on the brain's "doors," or receptors. They are not perfect messengers— they knock on every door until one opens. Some doors open to the messenger, and some don't. So imagine if you don't have enough doors that open along the road. If your serotonin messenger heads out with a "be happy" message but can't find enough doors to open, the brain slides into depression. Sometimes we simply don't have enough messengers "on the job," or the road they must travel is in disrepair, blocking the lifeline (circuit) between the thinking brain and the emotional brain.
- **Chronic stress.** When our stress response is stuck in "drive," it can actually change the structure, function, and

connectivity of regions in our brain. It's the same kind of impact that year-round severe weather has on a blacktop road—cracks and holes and disintegration can make the road impassible. Chronic stress can actually increase the brain's responsiveness to stress messages while decreasing its responsiveness to happy messages. The "construction crews" in our body chemistry add "lanes" to the busier highways, and the less-used roadways get neglected.

- **Head injuries.** Even hits that do not cause concussions, or mild traumatic brain injuries, can alter the brain's architecture, affecting the way it functions. At the Amen Clinics, we have found that a significant proportion of our patients' symptoms are influenced by a past head injury.
- **Inflammation.** As we've already noted, an increase in inflammatory markers in the anterior cingulate cortex (ACC) and other limbic structures can significantly impair our ability to assess and efficiently manage anxious thoughts. Inflammation has been identified in the postmortem studies of people who died by suicide and in the blood and cerebrospinal fluid of people who struggle with suicidal ideation or have a history of violent or high-intent suicide attempts.
- **Other direct or indirect insults to the brain.** A wide variety of other "brain toxins" can alter the brain's architecture and lead to threat-response dysfunction. They include substance abuse, infections, toxin exposure, nutritional deficits, hormonal (thyroid) deficits, and chronic medical illnesses.

4. **Individual and environmental variables can increase the risk of suicide, especially when they're mixed into a "cocktail" of circumstances.**

When both personal and circumstantial variables pile on top of each other, they can create a "perfect storm" that overwhelms a person's normal defenses. For example, let's say a "negative life event" such as divorce intrudes into the life of a person whose social/behavioral/resilience skills are compromised. If that person has also been over-exposed to suicide in the media or in his or her family, and if he or she has had previous psychiatric struggles or brain illnesses, the "perfect storm" is building. Add to these factors a history of substance abuse and ready access to lethal means (guns, medications, or illicit drugs, for example) and the person can feel caught in a hurricane.

Negative life events can include:

- A stressful family environment
- Parent-child conflicts
- Unrealistic and overwhelming parental expectations that lead to persistent feelings of failure
- Family rejection that is tied to sexual orientation (a whopping 900 percent increased risk)
- Exposure to the suicidal behavior of family members or in the media (this is commonly called "suicide contagion"—it's tied to identification with and modeling of suicidal behavior that is normalized by repeated exposure and detailed reporting)
- Child abuse (physical and sexual) leading to post-traumatic stress disorder, depression, and suicidal behavior
- Homelessness and corresponding exposure to abuse, violence, drugs, and alcohol
- A history of foster care
- The loss of a romantic relationship or the loss of a parent

- Bullying (as a victim or perpetrator), harassment, and victimization—the risk factor is worse if it's related to sexual orientation
- Legal or financial problems
- Overwhelming expectations or challenges at school or work
- Health challenges that involve chronic pain

Previous psychiatric struggles or brain illnesses are factors because one or more psychiatric diagnoses are evident in nine out of ten suicides.[6]

- The most common diagnoses are depression, bipolar disorder, schizophrenia/psychosis, anxiety, conduct disorder, and substance abuse disorders.
- Multiple diagnoses significantly increase the risk.
- Substance abuse (heroin, methamphetamine, steroids, and alcohol) is associated with suicidal ideation and planning, as well as actual attempts.
- Aggressive-impulsive behavior increases the risk.
- Hopelessness and pessimism both increase the risk.
- Prior suicide attempts are one of the strongest predictors of subsequent attempts and suicide deaths.

Access to lethal means is primarily tied to firearms:[7]

- Firearms contribute to nearly half of all completed suicides, likely because suicides carried out with a gun appear to be more impulsive and lethal compared to other methods.
- In an analysis of CDC data by the group Everytown for Gun Safety, researchers found that the rate of

firearm suicides increased by 51 percent for fifteen-to-twenty-four-year-olds in the decade ending in 2018. And among ten-to-fourteen-year-olds (traditionally a lower rate of suicide), gun-related suicides increased a staggering 214 percent.[8]

- Gun suicide attempts are remarkably lethal, compared to all other means. When no firearm is involved, most suicide attempts fail (94 percent), and most of those attempts are not repeated. But when a gun is used in the attempt, 90 percent succeed.[9]

- Living in a state with high overall gun ownership increases the risk of suicide (generally, states with the highest percentage of gun owners also have the highest rates of attempted and completed suicide). For each 10-percent increase in household gun ownership in a state, the suicide rate for ten-to-nineteen-year-olds increases by more than 25 percent.[10]

- Living in a home where guns are present is a key factor (in homes of youth who die by suicide, gun ownership is five times more prevalent).

Family-based genetic and environmental dysfunctions increase the risk.

- A family is a "forming" environment, of course—but biology also plays a huge role (the same way obesity is the result of both a cognitive/learned lifestyle and also genetic components).

- There is evidence that risk of suicide is tied to a parent's brain health issues (for example, the incidences of suicide are higher in aggressive-impulsive families).

- Lower levels of serotonin in the brain often produce increased serotonin receptors to compensate for the deficit, and that impacts emotion regulation, stress tolerance, resilience, and cognition.

- A lower number of glucocorticoid receptors in the prefrontal cortex and amygdala undermines stress tolerance and resilience.

- Abnormal activity in the temporal lobe, measured by a SPECT scan that tracks changes in activity level via blood-flow patterns in the brain, is related to poor regulation of aggressive feelings.

- Decreased activity in the PFC, which is visible in a SPECT scan, undermines one's ability to regulate impulsive actions—which is particularly dangerous when combined with unregulated aggressive impulses.

How Do "Destructive Narratives" Grow and Operate?

Software and hardware problems in the brain work in tandem to cement internal narratives that grow like toxic viruses inside us. This is a "Which came first, the chicken or the egg?" conundrum—our destructive narratives (caused by software "bugs") change the structural, functional, and neurochemical makeup of our brain, but alterations in the brain's structure, function, and neurochemical makeup (caused by genetics or injury) impact our ability to run healthy software.

On day, during a fitness class that I (Rick) take twice a week, the instructor fixated on the word "believe" in the workout song that was blasting from the speakers, then bellowed this warning: "Whatever you believe may come true, so you better believe something good!" (Out of the mouths of fitness instructors...)

Our beliefs, it's true, do shape our reality. And it's not because they have magic Harry Potteresque powers. No, we become the things we believe about ourselves because our beliefs are inextricably linked to our interior narratives, and the "editor" of our interior narratives is like the mythological centaur—half psychology (or software) and half biology (or hardware).

Michael Warden, president of the Ascent Coaching Group, writes: "We are an innately narrative species. It's impossible for us to perceive the universe outside of the context of story. We understand things and people by constructing stories around them to explain them to ourselves. Our stories tell us who we are. Or maybe it's more accurate to say it this way: We become defined by the stories we tell ourselves."

This insight is especially true when our defining stories remain hidden from our "conscious radar"—when we defend them even when they are destructive to us. "And yet," says trauma counselor Chris Bruno, "when these stories have been shaped by the traumatic experience of living in this broken world, it is by these stories that we actually survive. The abused child truly cannot trust, and by not trusting has found some measure of safety. The one who experiences rejection has learned to push people away first to survive the rejection. We live out these stories, most often, because they are both true and protective of our broken hearts. The story of how we found safety while immersed in danger speaks to the soul's inventive brilliance. And yet, when we continue to live out of these destructed narratives for our own self-protection, we find that they, too, destroy our ability to connect to others."[11]

These narrative ruts, produced by our "bugged" hardware and software in tandem, have the effect of turning the strong protective mechanisms we use to defend ourselves against outside threats in on ourselves—like a soldier pointing his gun at his own head instead of the enemy. And so...

- If the story you are telling about yourself interprets the abuse you endured as a child as overwhelming evidence that no one can be trusted, then you will live your life trusting no one, including the God who longs to redeem you, because that validates your story.
- If the story you are telling about yourself is that you have always been an outsider, someone the "insiders" habitually ignore, then you will live your life unconsciously pushing people away because that validates your story.
- If the story you are telling about yourself is that you are very difficult to love and that others can be coerced into loving you only when you perform perfectly for them, then you will live your life as a perfectionist, performing for people who never seem satisfied by your standards because that validates your story.
- If the story you are telling about yourself is that your life has a kind of cancerous effect on others, even on those who insist they love you, then taking your own life eventually makes rational sense and validates your story.

But...if the story you are telling about yourself is defined by the radical reality spoken by Jesus to His disciples on the eve of their first missionary journey, then you are "free indeed": "What is the price of two sparrows—one copper coin? But not a single sparrow can fall to the ground without your Father knowing it. And the very hairs on your head are all numbered. So don't be afraid; you are more valuable to God than a whole flock of sparrows" (Matthew 10:29–30).

We can live in freedom from fear, Jesus is telling us, if we will accept and embrace and ingest the belief that we are inestimably valuable to Him. And when this truth becomes the bedrock truth of our narrative, we validate His story. Of course, the deceptive narratives that we have already embraced are at war with this truth, so we give it our "good Christian" lip service—that we might actually be seen as a priceless treasure to God often seems impossible to truly embrace.

We are all held captive to the things we believe about ourselves—this is why Jesus warns us: "Your eye is like a lamp that provides light for your body. When your eye is healthy, your whole body is filled with light." And to reiterate His warning: "But when your eye is unhealthy, your whole body is filled with darkness. And if the light you think you have is actually darkness, how deep that darkness is!" (Matthew 6:22–23). If the eye is the window into the soul, the pupil is—quite literally—an opening into the eye. The pupil acts like the aperture on a camera, dilating or contracting to regulate the amount of light coming into the eye. Psychologists consider pupil dilation to be an honest cue to sexual or social interest. That's because pupil size isn't under our voluntary control.[12] Let's say you're trying to fake interest as your coworker recounts every stroke in his weekend golf game. You can force a smile. You might even remember to crinkle the corners of your eyes to make that smile look real. But your tiny pupils will reveal your lack of interest.

An "unhealthy eye" is an interior narrative that is telling a lie, not a truth, about us. And this is how we get stuck in a rut. We embrace lies that seem true about us, then we spend our life proactively (but often unconsciously) gathering evidence that seems to prove that these lies are true. Our destructive narratives feed on themselves, propelled forward by both our biology and our psychology. In other words, our life experiences can create and nourish unhealthy self-narratives (faulty software), leading to hopelessness about who we are and what our future will be like. This chronic process, in turn, changes the structural, functional, and neurochemical makeup of the brain.

Escaping the "Death Spiral"

Our way out of "the valley of the shadow of death" is a journey. Along the way, we'll need both software and hardware strategies to guide us. And that makes sense, because we are whole people, not compartmentalized. This is why in Matthew 9, Jesus first forgives the paralyzed man of his sins (his spiritual paralysis) before He heals him of his physical problem; to Jesus, software problems are just as important as hardware problems. We find freedom when we challenge the foundations of the self-stories that are keeping us captive. Chris Bruno offers three questions that help us surface and assess our internal narratives:

- What is the story I wish to live?
- Are my methods of survival, which have truly saved my life thus far, still saving me?
- What might now be possible that was not possible when I first experienced harm?[13]

In addition, other "outside assets" can help us stop spinning our wheels and pull us out of our rut:

- An emotionally involved and supportive family
- Parental or sibling support
- A family that "sees" and accepts and welcomes
- Strong relational connections at school or work, fueled by perceived safety (for example, anti-bullying and anti-harassment policies)
- Strong relational connections at church or in the community
- Reduced access to lethal means (firearms, pesticides, and pills, for example)
- Stronger learned social and behavioral skills, leading to greater resilience (a positive self-concept and view of the future)
- Growth and increased mastery in good decision-making, problem solving, healthy adaptive coping (shrinking the

incidence of maladaptive coping such as self-harm, drug
use, and unhealthy sexual practices)

For the vast majority of us, the good news is that most of these outside factors that can influence our stuckness are within our control. Of course, we'll need to be intentionally managing and maintaining our hardware and software; "magical" solutions simply don't exist. And the practices and strategies we reveal and explore in this book will directly address our "agency," or our ability to follow Jesus up from the valley into the light. For those of us who must confront the "dragging" influence of our biology, there is significant hope for a healthy future if we'll face our challenges with a collaborative mindset and nurture intentional practices that address both hardware and software bugs.

CHAPTER 2

UNDERSTANDING OUR STORY

**How Story Works to Construct, Give Meaning to,
and Set Boundaries around Our Reality and How the
Stories We Embrace about Ourselves Can Become
"Weaponized"**

We've said the software operating system for human beings is also called our "story." And we've emphasized that our whole health is profoundly influenced by the interior narrative we cultivate, accept, and embrace about ourselves. A healthy, authentic, and God-conscious interior narrative is a bulwark against a gravitational pull toward suicidality. And a corrupted, self-cannibalizing interior narrative propels us toward "terminal velocity"—a descent into darkness that is difficult to slow.

Not long ago, I (Rick) had coffee with a friend who'd recently planted a church. He was in the early stages of trying to bring together a community of people who were committed to living out their authentic stories in the glaring light of intentional relationships. Casey was wrestling over the tension created by his vision for authentic community—of course, this would require vulnerability, and that's a minefield for almost everyone. On the way home after our conversation, Casey couldn't stop thinking about the challenges facing the people who had been drawn to his vision but struggled to be vulnerable as they wrestled against the gravitational pull of their shattered and traumatized stories. Here's the note he wrote me after he got home:

> People outside the church expect people who are inside the church to have it together. So, when we talk to our neighbors or friends we're a little insecure about letting people know what it's really like on "the inside." Do we "blow our witness" by letting other broken people know how broken we really are?
>
> Western culture, and especially our Western Christian culture, covertly pushes us into image-maintenance mode. It's especially hard for people to discover that leaders and pastors have struggles or issues or difficulties, because there's an implied expectation of relative perfection. And when we struggle with doubt or weakness, we worry that it'd be devastating for others if it ever got out.
>
> In our performance-based culture and perfection-obsessed society, we all put our best foot forward in relationships—this system is based on covering up our faults, weaknesses, and insecurities. We all play the game—knowing we don't have it all together but trying to make sure that everyone else thinks we do.
>
> But what if we had the courage to embrace a kind of raw authenticity that was embedded within a redemptive reality? What if we valued knowing the scars, wounds, and struggles of others, because we had a sacred respect for how those things have shaped them into a force to be reckoned with? What if we all had an increasing freedom to be who we really are, tell it like it really is, and "out" our shortcomings and failures for what they really are? That would be a strange, messed-up, and liberated world....[1]

Casey's hypotheticals emphasize both the hope and the challenge of "outing" the struggles that catalyze our destructive narratives. These psychological IEDs are often buried deep, and they're best defused by the "bomb squad" that is a healthy, functioning Christian community. Sometimes these explosive self-stories detonate before they can be detected, and sometimes the "collateral damage" harms those close to us. And sometimes the bomb squad counts the cost and decides the risk is not worth the effort it will take to defuse the "explosives" lurking under a person's surface. People in this situation feel isolated from community even when they appear well-connected on the surface. Our hardware issues (genetic malfunctions, chronic stress, head injuries, inflammation, and other brain toxins) and software issues (cognitive distortions, hopelessness, negative self-evaluations, and dire predictions for the future) conspire to undermine and weaponize our interior narrative, twisting what author William Paul Young calls "the truth of our being" into a time-release incendiary that can blow up our identity.

In the shocking slipstream of fashion designer Kate Spade's suicide, her longtime friend and business partner Elyce Arons told a reporter: "Katy was very happy most of the time, the funniest person in the world, and sometimes she would get really sad.... We would talk a lot about [Spade's depression], and end up laughing. She really felt she could power through it on her own." Arons remembers talking about suicide with Spade whenever there was news of a celebrity death: "She'd say to me, 'I would never do that. I would never do that. I would never do that,' and I believed her." Spade's husband, Andy, told the *New York Times*: "There was no indication and no warning that she would do this. It was a complete shock. And it clearly wasn't her. There were personal demons she was battling."[2]

Though "personal demons" is a metaphor, it's closer to accurate than we assume. Our weaponized self-stories carry a demonic impact; they have the ability to "steal, kill, and destroy" (John 10:10) our true identity if left buried and unchecked.

Jesus is a "brutal realist"—His redemptive intent in our life eschews rose-colored glasses. He will not try to "spin" our traumas and wounds into a happy façade. He will take exactly what was meant to destroy us and "MacGyver" it into a wellspring of life. This is a truth about God that Joseph discovered the hard way. Listen to him explain God's inventive brilliance to the brothers who first imprisoned him, then sold him as a slave, shattering his life: "You intended to harm me, but God intended it all for good. He brought me to this position so I could save the lives of many people" (Genesis 50:20). Like Joseph:

- We have an enemy whose aim is to recruit us as willing partners in the demolition of our identity.
- This enemy wants to use our brutal realities to warp our interior narratives into "weapons of mass destruction."
- These narratives are planted along our path, ready to detonate.

But God, as Joseph explains to his brothers, is like a martial artist—He uses the intent and momentum of our opponent against him, encouraging the growth of nourishing fruit in our soul. He will plant the "tree" of our identity in the manure of our circumstances, turning our traumas and losses and disappointments and betrayals and defeats into the sort of "rich soil" that transforms a seed into a fruit tree.

James, the brother of Jesus, launches his epistle with this: "Consider it all joy, my brethren, when you encounter various trials, knowing that the testing of your faith produces endurance. And let endurance have its perfect result, so that you may be perfect and complete, lacking in nothing" (James 1:2). Wholeness is Jesus's end game with us—a "lacking in nothing" identity. And wholeness is tied to our bedrock understanding of who we are and what matters most to us. Jesus is the Master Gardener, recultivating a soul landscape that was once a minefield into a thriving garden. And the fruits of that garden will feed and sustain our relational "village." Yes, the African proverb "it takes a village to raise a child" is true in every culture. But the "village" is also our path into restoration and wholeness. Crises give us access to what is going on inside our soul, because they reveal where the IEDs are buried, exposing them so the bomb squad can help defuse them. This means we must make our core narratives available to others and to Jesus. And to give others access to the stories we tell ourselves, we must first endeavor to understand them.

An Expedition into Story

Trauma counselor Chris Bruno says: "Every good story has four primary parts. Story begins with innocence, moves too quickly into tragedy, spends most of its time and focus on struggle, and ultimately seeks restoration. Reading your own story has power, but reading one another's stories sets captives free, binds up broken hearts, and proclaims the day of celebration."[3] We live inside our stories; they are either working to set us free from captivity or working to imprison us. Fielding Graduate University psychologist Pamela Rutledge offers these "psychological reasons why stories are so powerful":

1. Stories have always been a primal form of communication. They are timeless links to ancient traditions, legends, archetypes, myths, and symbols.

2. Stories are about collaboration and connection. Through stories we share passions, sadness, hardships and joys. We share meaning and purpose.... Stories allow us to understand ourselves better and to find our commonality with others.

3. Stories are how we think. They are how we make meaning of life. Call them schemas, scripts, cognitive maps,

mental models, metaphors, or narratives. Stories are how we explain how things work, how we make decisions, how we justify our decisions, how we persuade others, how we understand our place in the world, create our identities, and define and teach social values.

4. Stories provide order. Humans seek certainty and narrative structure is familiar, predictable, and comforting. Within the context of the story arc we can withstand intense emotions because we know that resolution follows the conflict. We can experience with a safety net.

5. Stories are how we are wired. Stories take place in the imagination. To the human brain, imagined experiences are processed the same as real experiences.

6. Stories are the pathway to engaging our right brain and triggering our imagination. By engaging our imagination, we become participants in the narrative. We can step out of our own shoes, see differently, and increase our empathy for others. Stories connect us and bridge differences.[4]

In a psychological context, our story (or self-narrative) plays a central role in our mental health. We are broken sojourners in a broken world, contested by an "enemy" and a "Victor" who understand that our identity is the battleground. We are caught up in this never-ending war as both collateral damage ("The dragon was angry at the woman and declared war against the rest of her children—all who keep God's commandments and maintain their testimony for Jesus"[Revelation 12:17]) and beloved children of a King ("But to all who believed him and accepted him, he gave the right to become children of God" [John 1:12]).

Because our identity is the fulcrum of our life—the point at which we "tip" toward wholeness or self-destruction—our "narrative self" (the fuel of our identity) needs caretaking. Rutgers University professor

Elisabeth Camp says: "We're fundamentally sense-making creatures—'homo narrans,' as John Niles puts it—'tellers' instead of homo sapiens or 'knowers.' On a narrative view, who I am is given by the story I tell about myself. Or, maybe, to guard against rampant self-deception by the story that an especially honest version of myself would tell. Think about the sorts of things we tell each other on first dates and at parties and in our memoirs: Where we come from, what's happened to us so far, where we are headed. When I ask myself 'Who am I?' I'm asking how to shape the story of my life so it hangs together into a meaningful, well-rounded whole."[5]

From a clinical perspective, our life experiences (lessons from our parents, observations, and personal experiences) help us construct a self-narrative that helps us make sense of our reality. This "making sense of" is vital to how we process our:

- Inherent value
- Expectations
- Goals
- Problem-solving
- Mental flexibility
- Optimism
- Positive self-concept

You probably know people in your life who seem like they were born with some of these attributes—and that's likely true. But we also learn them through "experiences that teach" and the modeling/nurturing of influential people in our lives. In general, negative life experiences create and nourish unhealthy self-narratives (bugged software). These "bugs" are hiding in plain sight—if your resilience skills are weak, or your lack of social awareness often pushes others away, or your default setting is a negative self-appraisal, or you repeatedly struggle to cope with challenges, or your first response to a threat is to narrate the story of your hopeless future—you're experiencing the outward markers of the bugs in your software, or self-narrative. And, just as it is true with your computer, the longer these identity viruses remain, the more likely they are to embed themselves as chronic distortions. Simply put, undiscovered IEDs become a part of your psychological landscape, changing the structural, functional, and neurochemical makeup of your brain (software changing hardware or psychology changing biology).

To surface these bugs in a clinical setting, we do "intake interviews" at Amen Clinics, asking clients to fill out questionnaires and submit to psychological testing. When we're face-to-face, our "narrative archeology" strategy is to quietly listen as they recount their personal history and describe their challenges and goals (and how they've interpreted them). We're looking for how they assess "their locus of control," and we want them to narrate why they're seeking help, what assumptions they've made about their recovery, and what they are hoping for. In addition, we're asking:

- Do they value themselves?
- Do they see themselves as empowered and able to impact their circumstances?
- How do they problem-solve (do they identify supports or seek help)?
- What expectations do they have for themselves?
- What is the nature of their spiritual practice?
- How do they treat others (do they show grace, for example)?

Problems that we uncover during this archaeological dig may reveal a narrative "lean" toward self-destructive ideation and behaviors. For example: "A lack of adequate problem-solving and a tendency to engage in problem-solving avoidance contribute to hopelessness and to negative evaluations about self and future, both of which are associated with greater suicide ideation. Because the individual avoids solving problems or has difficulty solving them, his or her stressors may be exacerbated, and he or she may therefore feel unable to improve his or her situation, leading to hopelessness and negative thoughts about self and future."[6] In a note from Ellie, a patient of Daniel's who had to pick her way through the rubble of her young life before emerging into a successful career as a nurse, the "narrative markers" that represent bugs in her software are clear:

> I am just reading through my journal that I've kept since 2017—the summer after I dropped out of school for the second time. I was working part-time and taking classes at the community college. In general, I was pretty miserable and had this insane tunnel vision on perfection. It's crazy to see how much I've grown.
>
> One thing I noticed was how constantly disgusted I was with myself around food—like I couldn't control myself. Since we switched to the [new medication], I haven't felt that way at all. Honestly, I think I am pretty resilient.... After reading some of the things I wrote about how terrible I thought I was, how lonely I was, how easy it would be to die, how I punished myself for imperfection—it just makes me more proud to be where I am. I'm about to graduate college with a 3.9 GPA, I now have so many friends who care about me, I'm more confident than I think I've ever been in my entire life, and I'm a pretty happy person. I really don't know how I did it. Reading some of the things I wrote makes me wonder what mysterious driving force inside me kept me going.
>
> I guess one thing I would tell my younger self is that no feeling is permanent. I always felt that whatever emotion I was experiencing was where I'd be stuck forever, but that's

really not the case. Bad feelings always pass even if they feel like they won't at the time. I feel like if I had believed that, it would have helped prevent suicide attempts that I made, because a lot of what fueled those attempts was the belief I would feel like a failure and feel awful forever, that there was no way out of what I was experiencing.

How Bugs Get Lodged in Our Story

Why do some appear to maintain a healthy interior "story" while others don't? Developing and maintaining a healthy self-narrative is a continuous process. We've said Jesus is a "Master Gardener," tilling the soil of our interior narrative and planting good seeds there. So think of tending to your self-narrative as if you were tending a garden. To grow anything in a garden, we do the following:

- Prep the soil
- Plant the seeds
- Water the plants
- Remove the weeds
- Harvest at the right time

Now, some of us are blessed with good soil and innate gardening skills (a "green thumb" mix of hardware and software). But some of us must rehabilitate our soil, enriching it with the "organic matter" it's missing. And some of us must learn the skills of gardening, since they don't come naturally to everyone. In either scenario, we need a basic gardening tool kit that is filled with the skills we need to grow things. Likewise, if we're going to grow a healthy interior narrative, we'll need to add a few basic skills to our psychological tool kit. One of the most important skills we'll need to develop is proficient problem-solving. Chronic distortion in this area of "narrative editing" is a clear risk factor for suicidality. If you're an "avoider" in life, we can spot risk indicators for this behavior in your basal ganglia using neuroimaging (a SPECT scan). That portion of your brain is responsible for many tasks, including managing the "dial" on your anxiety level. People who have a lot of activity in the basal ganglia tend to have a higher baseline level of anxiety. Anxiety is a tool. The brain generates it as a motivator of behavior or an alarm. The question is: How will you "use" that increased activity level? Will it activate an adaptive coping strategy (facing the challenge) or a maladaptive one (avoiding the challenge)? These are fundamental problem-solving decisions we make early in life. Because they're decisions, this avoidance response sounds volitional—but it's not, or at least not completely.

Think about how we learn to walk—we start out stumbling, but we learn from our experiences how to keep doing what works for us and stop doing what doesn't work. This is mostly an automatic process initiated by our volition. Eventually, through trial and error, we manage to stay on our feet as we move forward. In the same way, if avoiding seems to work for us early in life, then we keep doing it until our response feels "locked in" or habitual. At this point our biology has changed. The brain will begin to reward habitual behavioral patterns that it identifies as potentially helpful for survival (even if those patterns are incorrect or even harmful). When we see the storm coming, our brain generates anxiety, and we resolve to do something in response, so we build a shelter. And our brain rewards us for this progression. When we take care of our basic necessities—food, clothing, and shelter—the brain is "programmed" to perpetuate these behaviors with a reward response.

Occasionally, this reward response can be tied to maladaptive coping strategies, such as choosing to avoid thinking about the storm until the rain is coming down on you in sheets. The short-term reward is tied to temporarily sidelining our anxiety, but we're setting ourselves up for long-term pain when we ignore adequate preparations for challenging circumstances using procrastination behaviors—for example, waiting until the last minute to prepare for a test or a presentation or to complete your tax returns. The brain will continue to weigh the benefits of this decision-avoidance strategy versus its costs until a habitual response is reinforced. (Behaviors like this are related to attention-deficit/hyperactivity disorder, general anxiety, or both). Furthermore, our "rewarder" can become compromised, making our problem-solving lens distorted. In a research report published in *Molecular Psychiatry*, a team of psychiatrists discovered a clear link between "alterations" in our brain reward network and a weakened ability to choose between "a smaller immediate reward versus a larger but delayed reward, especially when the two rewards were more than one year apart...potentially undermining the deterrents and the generation of alternative solutions during a suicidal crisis."[7] Translated, this means that the brain promotes the immediate relief of suicide over the long-term reward of further battling through the pain in a vulnerable brain. Ellie proves this dynamic in her story: "Bad feelings always pass."

This means that some people who are battling stuck narratives and a downward pull toward darkness have a biological deficit that hinders their ability to move into and through their potholes—they spin their wheels over and over (because it promises an immediate reward) rather than do the work needed to successfully move the car out of the hole with a delayed-reward strategy (finding some tree limbs to jam under the tires and digging away at the rim of the pothole to make it easier to exit).

So, when we repeat an early coping technique and/or experience biological alterations in our brain's coping tools, that road full of potholes might masquerade as a hopeless trap, not simply a challenging stretch of road. This is where our interior narrative either helps us keep moving or stalls us. In other words, to make sense of our circumstances ("Here I am, stuck again"), we embrace a narrative that leans either toward "hopeless trap" or "challenging stretch." Then we look for evidence that supports our existing narrative—we're never looking for evidence that will refute the story we've already embraced and defended. This is called "selective attention." Once we've bought into a certain narrative, we're only going to look for supporting evidence. So, if you're a runner and you see yourself as an "elite" front-runner, you'll work to maintain your front-runner status because that will reinforce your narrative. If you're a runner who struggles at the back of the pack, and you see yourself as a marginal athlete, you'll find supporting evidence to stay at the back. To break free from a "stuck narrative," you need experiences that conflict with the evidence you've already gathered through selective attention. You need to finish the race in a much higher place, for example, than your interior narrative says is possible for you. Now that narrative is suspect, because its premise has been challenged through experience—if you choose to embrace this new evidence.

These tendencies are not "set" in our brains for the rest of our lives—it's just that, broadly speaking, people identify with a "solving" or "avoiding" response to problems and challenges. And the story we're telling ourselves furthers both responses. The story we tell ourselves about ourselves is like a fast-running river—once our canoe is in the water, the current will take us where the water is flowing. We can paddle as hard as we want, but ultimately, we must recognize where the current is likely to take us and get the help we need to move our canoe into a different stream—if the current is not leading us to the destination we want.

- Does that thought help you feel better or worse?
- If it makes you feel worse, why do you choose to hold on to it?
- If you let go of that thought, what new thought can you pick up and "own"?

For some of us, the "fast-running river" that is carrying our canoe forward is leading to a two-hundred-foot waterfall. Staying in that river means we're progressing toward a "non-survivable hazard." So our "end game" is simple: Write our own narrative, inviting Jesus to be our co-author. And if Jesus is helping us write our story, He will not include "non-survivable hazards," and He will provide a path of escape if we get caught in the wrong current. Paul reminds us: "The temptations in your life are no different from what others experience. And God is faithful. He will not allow the temptation to be more than you can stand. When you are tempted, he will show you a way out so that you can endure" (1 Corinthians 10:13). And Jesus is blunt about His narrative intent: "The thief's purpose is to steal and kill and destroy. My purpose is to give them a rich and satisfying life" (John 10:10).

In Part Two, we'll explore exactly what this "co-authoring" life looks like from a wide variety of perspectives and practices. But if we know selective attention is a powerful default setting in all of us, the most important thing we can do is choose well what we selectively attend to, thus building and embracing an interior narrative that leads to life, not death.

Ted's Story

I was pastor of the fastest-growing church in my denomination, a magnet for people who loved Jesus but didn't like religion. The church was bursting at the seams, quickly growing from twenty-five members to more than five hundred in less than two years. I was traveling around the country, meeting with big-time church leaders who praised me for my leadership and studied my "model." But no one suspected the secret I was guarding—my success was camouflaging a destructive interior storyline that would later threaten all my relationships and the church community I'd worked so hard to plant.

My high school classmates voted me the class clown; that means I learned how to be an expert at making them laugh. Nothing fed my soul's need for affirmation more than people-pleasing. Later in college, I painted a self-portrait—a weeping clown. On the outside I was a stand-up comic (not a metaphor—I actually was a stand-up comic), but I was using humor to stave off the grief and shame and anxiety and the leaking hole at the bottom of my identity. I was convinced that my ability to delight and amuse was the only thing that made my life matter. I was addicted to people-pleasing. Later, I shifted to a "harder drug"— humor couldn't fully hide my interior reality, so I turned to bulimia. I embraced the destructive narrative that my body image would win me the respect and admiration I craved. So I secretly managed my physical appearance by forcing myself to throw up the food I'd just eaten.

My "success" exposed a toxin in my soul—I had little confidence in my own heart. My convictions were more like reactions, fueling a relational style that was like Velcro—if you got close enough to me, I'd get my hooks in you and become enmeshed. I couldn't mark the boundary line between my identity and your identity. I "led" by finding out what people wanted, then trying to give it to them. Sooner or later, that's a recipe for relational destruction; the story I was trying to live inside would threaten to rip all my relationships apart in the end.

Meanwhile, our rapid growth gave me the excuse I needed to ignore my urgent need for change, but behind the façade my life was accelerating into destruction. A year or two into our church plant, my son was quickly descending into drug abuse, petty crime, and disruptive behavior at school and home. We found a counselor who told us the problem was rooted in my son's inability to control his emotional escalations. And so our mission in life shifted to managing the triggers that led to our son's escalations. It was people-pleasing and relational enmeshment on a desperate level. And it didn't work. So we found a new counselor, who quickly listed the obvious mistakes I was making. Over the course of our appointments, he told us that our whole family, led by my example, had fallen into a systemic rut. His diagnosis, centering on me as the hub of the problem, made me (understandably) defensive and resistant to input. I thought: *How can this be? I'm the hero of this story.*

Slowly, as I allowed myself to admit that I was the driving force in our family's dysfunction, I descended into a deep despair. I hated who I was. And I couldn't keep myself from hurting the people I cared for most. I was spiraling down into the darkness, propelled by a killer self-story masquerading as my identity.

We managed, against my son's violent objections, to get him into a long-term therapy facility. Now, with him temporarily removed from the family system—the covering fog of his distractions cleared—the real culprit was left standing alone, naked and ashamed. In the midst of this agony, I was forced to confront my own enmeshed behavior. I had launched a fast-growing and much-admired church with a conviction—that the grace of Jesus overshadowed all other truths. And now, standing in the wreckage of my dysfunctional leadership, I knew I would either have to trust His grace or collapse under the weight of my self-narrative.

I once heard the story of a daughter stuck in her second-floor bedroom as her family's house burned down around her. She appeared at her bedroom window, with her father standing below, begging her to jump. But because of the thick smoke engulfing the home, she refused: "I can't see you, Daddy!" The father responded with calm assurance: "That's okay, honey, I can see you. Now jump!" And she did. Would I, like that little girl, jump from a burning house into the darkness of a promise? How could a man so disabled by his own interior narrative, and so dysfunctionally enmeshed with the agendas of others, emerge into the light?

"Humanly speaking," says Jesus, "it is impossible. But with God everything is possible" (Matthew 19:36). Now, as the "real me" begins to emerge, I recognize that my most powerful giftings are tied to the redemptive fruits of my narrative "accusers," who've now been exposed and de-fanged in me.... Yes, what my enemy (the enemy of God, and my own established ways of colluding with him) intended for evil, God is using for good....

CHAPTER 3

DEBUGGING OUR OPERATING SYSTEM

How "Wholly Living" Is the Key to a Healthy, Suicide-Resistant Personal Ecosystem

When He was old enough to understand, little Yeshua's Jewish parents told Him the fantastical story of His birth and how a repressive occupying regime, led by a paranoid madman, had targeted Him for execution while He was still a toddler. The madman's advisors warned him of the threat this little boy represented to his future power, so the ruler ordered the extermination of all boys under the age of two. Yeshua's family grabbed what they could and raced to flee the wave of violence before it washed over them. Many did not escape, and dozens of innocent children were ripped from their parents' arms and murdered in front of them. Yeshua's "birthday story" was shocking, gruesome, and traumatic.

And so, the little boy grew up in Egypt, a refugee in a foreign land where His parents scratched and sacrificed to scrape by. They were second-class citizens, systemically denigrated and disregarded. Eventually, after the madman's death, the family risked everything to return to their hometown. They saw neighbors and friends who'd lost their little boys to the purge and knew little Yeshua had been the target.

Tension over His impact and identity was often thick. He was not like
the other boys in town. He was precocious but never arrogant, hard-
working but not driven, curious and bold and at peace with Himself.
Some were drawn to Him; others were repelled by Him (including His
own brothers).

Later, after He had taken over his father's carpentry business and
was well-established in the community, He decided to leave all that
behind and take to the road as an itinerant rabbi, living off the generosity of strangers and gathering followers along the way. He spoke and
acted with authority, and that evoked both awe and withering abuse.
His critics kept up a perpetual stream of the latter—a determined
assault on His identity, using weaponized lies in an attempt to plant
destructive "bugs" in his "operating system."

- "You're a law-breaker!" (Matthew 12:1–14)
- "You're a glory-hound!" (John 7:4)
- "You get your power from Satan!" (Matthew
  12:22–37)
- "You must perform to prove your worth!" (Matthew
  12:38–45)
- "You're a blasphemer!" (John 10:33)
- "You're disrespectful!" (John 18:22)
- "You must conform to our expectations!" (Matthew
  16:21–28)
- "Who do you think you are?" (Matthew 21:23–46)

These assaults and traumas are, of course, powerful enough to
undermine and destabilize any normal person's identity. The "mir-
rors" that reflected back how others were experiencing Him, along
with His own dark backstory, had the power to drive Him into a
dark cave of despair. And Yeshua (Jesus's name in Aramaic, likely
how He most often heard it) was targeted by this toxic stream of

abuse for three years—every day, every hour. So how did He maintain the health of His hardware/software core and fend off the killer bugs others attempted to plant in His interior narrative? Our Sunday school answer is simple: *Well, Jesus is God—these assaults wouldn't impact Him the way they would impact me.* But a more interesting and biblically pertinent answer is: He lived a "wholly" life. Not just "holy," but "wholly."

A lifestyle of wholeness, as modeled by Jesus, helps us to expose, fend off, and eradicate bugs in our operating system, keeping our core identity intact and resistant to the identity assaults that trigger stuck narratives. Another way of describing this lifestyle is hardware/software maintenance that nurtures a healthy, suicide-resistant personal ecosystem, or a "wholly way to live." Simply, we more and more embrace a way of living that:

- Continually refines our "organizing principle" (a foundational belief system that guides our outlook on the world, our self-story, and our value, resilience, passion, and purpose)
- Nurtures a healthy thought life that matches our values
- Invests in a healthy lifestyle that maintains the "temple home" of God
- Catalyzes our creativity
- Forges healthy relational connections
- Contributes to our community
- Pursues an intentional, Jesus-centered life

Understanding Our Narrative Code

Because we're focusing in this chapter on debugging the human operating system, we must first explore strategies that will help us understand and identify our narrative "code." We can't change what we are unable to measure. And that means we must take inventory of how we think to understand why we think the ways we do so we can move toward a suicide-resistant way of thinking.

At the Amen Clinics, we use screeners and questionnaires to spotlight a person's self-narrative. The purpose of these tools is to help patients root out and identify their destructive belief systems and patterns of thinking—the unhealthy biases that are insidious (meaning they have subtle but profound momentum in our lives) in their impact, though we may not be fully aware of them or the severity of their influence on us.

Awareness itself is an intervention because the darkness is not our friend.

Coaxing our default storylines out of the darkness (buried under our shame and ignorance and coping mechanisms) and into the light of awareness has an innate power to drain those destructive narratives of the fuel they need to survive and thrive.

Again, Jesus emphasizes: "For everything that is hidden will eventually be brought into the open, and every secret will be brought to light. Anyone with ears to hear should listen and understand" (Mark 4:22–23). And why will "every secret be brought to light"? Conventionally, we assume Jesus is promising to "catch us" in our hidden sin—to "tattle" on us to the other members of the Trinity. But this is a low interpretation of His great and good heart. Jesus wants to surface our secret beliefs and self-narratives expressly because they are insidious and deeply influential. This process of awareness—bringing every hidden thing into the open—is an intervention, in the same way that exposing toxic molds to sunlight thwarts their poisonous impact.

Lindsay Christensen, a clinical nutritionist, health researcher, and writer, says: "During my late teens and early twenties, I suffered from an unexplainable chronic illness that significantly reduced my quality of life. I eventually learned that the illness I was experiencing had been caused by two primary factors—a Lyme infection and exposure to toxic mold in a previously water-damaged apartment building I had lived in. While I tried many different medications, supplements, and treatments for these illnesses, there is one therapy in particular that I found to be unexpectedly helpful—sunbathing!"[1] Christensen goes on to explain how a move from the Midwest to Colorado, which boasts more than three hundred days of sunshine every year, led to an accidental discovery: "The therapeutic use of light is effective in the treatment of fungal infection." And here's why this "nature-based" discovery is so important:

Jesus thinks and acts metaphorically because He is always trying to translate what is true in the Kingdom of God into language, images, and narratives that make sense to us in "the kingdom of our world." In Romans 1, Paul reveals the metaphoric intent God has planted in all of creation: "[Wicked people] know the truth about God because he has made it obvious to them. For ever since the world was created, people have seen the earth and sky. Through everything God made, they can clearly see his invisible qualities—his eternal power and divine nature. So they have no excuse for not knowing God" (Romans 1:19–20). Paul is describing the way patterns and truths in nature point to patterns and truths in our natural/spiritual life. Every aspect of the created world is embedded with clues to the "invisible" patterns of God's way of life. We will find them if we choose to pay attention. And Christensen's discovery about the power of sunlight in her battle against the influence of toxic mold on her health is a metaphor embedded in creation that reveals one of the Kingdom of God's truths: We must expose our story to the light if we want to undermine the impact of our toxic interior narratives. They grow in the dark, and they could kill us if left unchecked. Sunlight (or awareness) takes away the conditions these molds (our destructive self-stories) need to survive.

Intervention, then, means we become aware of our unhealthy thought patterns and then actively and safely unveil them to others as we work to change them. Dragging these narratives into the light not only exposes them to a "detoxifying agent," but also allows the same light that kills the growth of destructive narratives in us to promote the growth of healthy narratives. To paraphrase James, the brother of Jesus: "So humble yourselves before God [expose your narratives to the light]. Resist the devil [the destructive narratives God's enemy uses to 'kill, steal, and destroy'], and he will flee from you [the toxins will be neutralized]. Come close to God [expose yourself to the light], and God will come close to you [so you are 'infected' with healthy growth]" (James 4:7–8).

American psychologist Jeffrey Young has developed an integrative approach to surfacing our awareness of toxic narratives—ways of thinking that we have embraced so completely that they sometimes develop into chronic personality disorders. Young's approach is called schema therapy (ST). It is distinct from traditional approaches in several ways. The ST strategy:

- Highlights the way our current toxic-narrative symptoms have developed over time
- Emphasizes the narrative impact of the therapist–patient relationship and its potential for corrective influence
- Aims to help us understand our core emotional needs and learn ways of meeting those needs adaptively
- Focuses extensively on the processing of memories of aversive childhood experiences, using experiential techniques to alter negative emotions related to these memories[2]

As Young has explored this innovative therapy more deeply, he and his collaborators have built a growing menu of "maladaptive schemas." These are personal storylines that emerge from necessary (but twisted) responses to trauma in childhood. Formally, they are "broad, pervasive themes regarding oneself and one's relationship with others, developed during childhood and elaborated throughout one's lifetime, and dysfunctional to a significant degree." So far, Young and his colleagues have identified eighteen of these schemas. Go through the list that follows; spot your own "maladaptive" interior narratives, or "bugs" in your "computer code."

1. **Emotional Deprivation**—A default expectation that your desire for normal emotional support won't be adequately met by others. Three "branches" of deprivation include:

- Deprivation of Nurturance: An absence of attention, affection, warmth, or companionship
- Deprivation of Empathy: An absence of understanding, listening, self-disclosure, or mutual sharing of feelings from others
- Deprivation of Protection: An absence of strength, direction, or guidance from others

2. **Abandonment**—A perception that those whose role is to support us and offer us intimate connection are unstable and unreliable. It's the sense that our significant others will not be able to continue providing emotional support, connection, strength, or practical protection because they are emotionally unstable and unpredictable (for example, they have angry outbursts), unreliable, or erratically present. Also, when the important people in our lives are facing imminent death or seem willing to transfer their love and care to another, we wrestle with a self-narrative of abandonment.

3. **Mistrust**—The expectation that others will hurt, abuse, humiliate, cheat, lie, manipulate, or take advantage of us. The common perception is that the harm is intentional or the result of unjustified

and extreme negligence, and it may include the sense that we always "get the short end of the stick."

4. **Social Isolation/Alienation**—A pervading sense that we are isolated from the rest of the world, different from others, and/or not a welcomed member of any group or community.

5. **Defectiveness/Shame**—A feeling that there is something foundationally defective, bad, unwanted, inferior, or invalid about us, or that we'd be unlovable to significant others if they saw the truth about us. This schema often involves hypersensitivity to criticism, rejection, blaming behavior, self-consciousness, comparison thinking, and insecurity around others. These flaws may be attached to private characteristics (selfishness, angry impulses, unacceptable sexual desires) or public characteristics (undesirable physical appearance, social awkwardness).

6. **Failure**—A belief that we have already failed, or are sure to fail, or are fundamentally inadequate in comparison to our peers' achievements (school, career, sports, and so on). This schema often involves beliefs that we are stupid, inept, untalented, ignorant, lower in status, and simply less successful than others.

7. **Incompetence/Dependence**—A sense that we are unable to competently handle our everyday responsibilities without a great deal of help from others (for example, taking care of ourselves, solving daily problems, exercising good judgment, tackling new tasks, making good decisions). This schema often presents as helplessness.

8. **Vulnerability to Harm or Illness**—An exaggerated fear that a catastrophe will strike at any time and that we will be unable to prevent it. This fear focuses on one or more of these circumstantial threats: medical, emotional, or external catastrophes (for example, an elevator collapsing or victimization by criminals).

9. **Enmeshment**—A pattern of excessive emotional attachment and over-functioning with one or more significant others (often parents) at the expense of our distinct identity or normal social development.

This schema often involves the belief that at least one of the enmeshed individuals cannot survive or be happy without the constant support of the other. It may also include "smothering" feelings. It's often experienced as feelings of emptiness and floundering—our life seems to have no direction, and we may even question our own existence.

10. **Subjugation**—An excessive surrendering of control to others because we feel coerced into it, usually to avoid anger, retaliation, or abandonment. This schema usually involves a perception that our own desires, opinions, and feelings are not valid or important to others. Others experience us as excessively compliant, and we have a hypersensitivity to feeling trapped. This combination generally leads to a build-up of anger (passive-aggressive behavior, uncontrolled outbursts of temper, psychosomatic symptoms, withdrawal of affection, "acting out," and substance abuse). The two major forms of subjugation include:

- Subjugation of needs: we suppress our own preferences, decisions, and desires
- Subjugation of emotions: we suppress our own emotional expression, especially anger

11. **Self-Sacrifice**—An extreme focus on voluntarily meeting the needs of others in daily situations at the expense of our own gratification. The most common reasons we do this are to prevent causing pain to others, to avoid guilt from feeling selfish, or to maintain a connection with others we perceive as needy. This self-narrative often grows out of an acute sensitivity to the pain of others. Sometimes it leads to a sense that our own needs are not being adequately met, and we resent those who seem to enjoy the care we're missing. (This schema overlaps with the concept of codependency.)

12. **Emotional Inhibition**—Over-controlling our spontaneous actions, feelings, or communications. Usually, we do this to avoid

others' disapproval, feelings of shame, or the fear that we may lose control of our impulses. The most common areas of inhibition include the "editing" of:

- Anger and aggression
- Positive impulses (joy, affection, sexual excitement, play)
- Vulnerability and free communication of our feelings and needs
- "Irrationality" relative to our emotions

13. Unrelenting Standards—An underlying belief that we must strive to meet very high internalized standards of behavior and performance, usually to avoid criticism. This self-narrative typically results in pressured feelings and a difficulty in slowing down. Those who struggle with the implications of this schema are hypercritical toward themselves and others. And they are hampered in their ability to experience pleasure, relaxation, health, self-esteem, a sense of accomplishment, or satisfying relationships. The outward signs include:

- Perfectionism, involving an inordinate attention to detail and underestimating how good our own performance is relative to the "norm"
- Rigid rules and "shoulds" in many areas of life, including unrealistically high moral, ethical, cultural, or religious precepts
- Preoccupation with time and efficiency for the sake of "accomplishing more"

14. Entitlement/Superiority—A belief that we are superior to other people and therefore entitled to special rights and privileges; we are not bound by the rules of reciprocity that guide normal social interactions. In this schema, we insist on doing or having whatever we want regardless of what is realistic or reasonable, often at a cost to others. It may also be typified by an exaggerated focus on superiority (for example, we fashion ourselves as the "most" successful, famous, or wealthy) with a drive to achieve power or control (not primarily attention or approval). Sometimes this schema includes excessive competitiveness toward or domination of others without empathy or concern for their needs or feelings.

15. **Insufficient Self-Control/Self-Discipline**—A pervasive resistance to exercising self-control and tolerate frustration in pursuit of our goals, or to restrain excessive emotions and impulses. In its milder form, those who wrestle with this schema focus on discomfort-avoidance—that includes avoiding pain, conflict, confrontation, responsibility, or overexertion at the expense of personal fulfillment, commitment, or integrity.

16. **Admiration/Recognition-Seeking**—An overemphasis on gaining approval, recognition, or attention from other people—or a determination to fit in at the expense of developing a secure and true sense of self. In this schema, our sense of esteem depends on the reactions of others rather than on our own natural inclinations. It sometimes includes an overemphasis on status, appearance, social acceptance, money, or achievement as a means of gaining approval, admiration, or attention (not primarily for power or control). People who live within this schema frequently make major life decisions that are inauthentic or unsatisfying, and they are hypersensitive to rejection.

17. **Pessimism/Worry**—A pervasive, lifelong focus on the negative aspects of life (pain, death, loss, disappointment, conflict, guilt, resentment, unsolved problems, potential mistakes, betrayal, things that could go wrong, and so on) while minimizing or neglecting the positive or optimistic aspects. This schema usually fuels exaggerated expectations and the belief that things will eventually go seriously wrong, or that aspects of our life that seem to be going well will ultimately fall

apart. People who exhibit signs of this self-story have an inordinate fear of making mistakes that might lead to financial collapse, loss, humiliation, or getting trapped in a bad situation. Because potential negative outcomes are exaggerated, they are chronic worriers, over-vigilant, complain often, and struggle to make decisions.

18. **Self-Punitiveness**—A belief that we should be harshly punished for making mistakes. Those who exhibit this schema tend to be angry, intolerant, punitive, and impatient with others (including themselves) who do not meet expectations or standards. They usually struggle to forgive mistakes because of a reluctance to consider extenuating circumstances or human imperfection, and they have a hard time empathizing with others' feelings.[3]

Now, you probably "found yourself" in several of these schemas, not just one. And when you said to yourself, "That's me!" you are experiencing a subtle but profound intervention—an acknowledgment that your dysfunctional (and toxic) interior narratives have moved from the darkness into the light, where awareness can do its work. Light kills mold.

Debugging Our Narrative Code

Schemas are like lenses—through them, we see and understand the world. Metaphorically, they are the "eye" of our soul. They make up our cognitive structure, and they are built using the "blocks" of our prior knowledge and experiences. The eighteen schemas we've spotlighted here have an obvious harmful impact on us, but the good news is that healthy, adaptive schemas can produce rich fruit for us. Remember that favorite metaphor of Jesus's—that "if your eye is healthy, your whole body is full of light"? Well, here He describes how maladaptive schemas can be a threat to us: "So if your eye—even your good eye—causes you to lust, gouge it out and throw it away. It is better for you to lose one part of your body than for your whole body to be thrown into hell" (Matthew 5:29). Yes, "thrown into hell" seems like a reference to eternal punishment, but consider the impact of a maladaptive schema (a "bad eye") on the whole of your life. In the extreme, it can make your life a living hell. And Jesus's purpose, we know, is to "give [us] a rich and satisfying life" (John 10:10).

Harmful schemas are reinforced by cognitive distortions, which are consistent errors in our logic that contribute to erroneous conclusions, inaccurate perceptions of situations, and unhealthy interactions. Cognitive distortions develop from biased information-processing that is informed and fueled by one or more of these eighteen schemas. We look for information in situations and interactions that confirm our schemas and ignore evidence that challenges them. Even more dire, we will unconsciously choose situations that trigger our schemas and elicit responses from others that reinforce them. Because Charlotte,* an upper-middle-class suburban homemaker who lives in an affluent county on the West Coast, operates in the "Vulnerability to Harm or Illness" schema, she is constantly fretting about her family's financial future. Her husband makes a good living, they live in a beautiful home, they have three kids in college (one of them on a full-ride scholarship), and many obvious blessings. But Charlotte stresses about home repairs that may never be completed, pleasure travel that may never happen, and retirement savings that, she believes, won't be enough to keep them living above the poverty line. To an outside observer these fears are unfounded, but they are real to Charlotte—and because they are real, she spotlights the few bits of evidence that support her schema and ignores the mountain of evidence that contradicts it. As a result, Charlotte struggles to find hope in her life, and sometimes wonders if the world would be better off without her.

This is why it's important to identify our schemas and the cognitive distortions that perpetuate them. Because we live inside our schemas, it's difficult for us to identify them on our own. We often need the help of others, and we get the greatest level of precision when a clinician works to identify them. Once they are "outed," many cognitive distortions can be helped through short-term interventions. Examples of cognitive distortions include:

- All-or-nothing thinking (for example, that we have to be perfect or we're a complete and abject failure; there is no middle ground)
- Overgeneralizing (for example, if something bad happens just once, we expect it to happen over and over again)
- Discounting the positive (for example, when we see a single, unpleasant event as part of a never-ending pattern of defeat)
- Jumping to conclusions (for example, when we conclude that someone is holding a grudge against us, but we don't actually bother to find out if that's correct)
- Mind-reading (for example, we say we know what another person is feeling and thinking and exactly why they act the way they do)
- Fortune-telling (for example, when we believe our entire future is preordained)
- Magnification (catastrophizing) and minimizing (for example, when we expect disaster to strike, no matter what, or when we downplay our own strengths in comparison to another's strengths)
- Emotional reasoning (for example, simply because we feel stupid and boring we assume we must be stupid and boring)
- "Should" statements (for example, holding on to a list of ironclad rules about how every person should behave)
- Labeling and mislabeling (for example, when we tell ourselves "I'm a loser" after we've failed at a specific task)

- Personalization (for example, when we believe that everything others do or say is some kind of direct, personal reaction to us)

These cognitive distortions reinforce our negative schemas and influence our emotions and behavior. Once we've discovered and uncovered them, we are at a crossroads. What will we do with what has been surfaced in us? The key to debugging our software code is to identify and challenge these maladaptive schemas when we see them. We've said the first and primary intervention is awareness. But a bug in our story requires a solution that is story-based. This is why schema therapy hinges on offering the patient a "resolution story" that can guide the stuck person out of his or her dark place. The best way to envision this approach is to return to our pothole story and treat it like a fable.

I have managed to get my car stuck in a pothole again. I've tried hard to avoid these ruts—I'm steering through them the best I can. But, of course, here I am. No matter what, I always end up here. I thought I could just will my car out of this hole, but I'm just digging myself deeper into stuckness. I've seen people pass by who maybe could help, but no one seems that eager to stop for someone like me. Maybe they see how stuck I am and realize there's really nothing they can do. Or maybe my problem seems ridiculous to them. Or maybe I'm not even worth stopping for. Oh! If that is true, will I ever get out of this hole? Maybe it's time to finally abandon my car altogether...
   But who is this person approaching my car right now? He does not seem afraid or awkward or self-conscious like the others who've passed by. Is he here to help or...maybe to harm me even more? Can I trust him?

The Helper: Looks like you're really stuck—would you like some help?

Me: Oh yes, I've been stuck for a while, but I'm sure I can find my own way out.

The Helper: How did you find yourself in this situation?

Me: Well, it's not the first time—I guess I'm just a terrible driver. Getting stuck is probably inevitable for me.

The Helper: Well, this is a rough road—lots of people get stuck here. It looks like you've tried to get out on your own already, but that strategy hasn't worked very well. Would you be interested in my help? I think I know a path out of this hole that could really work.

Me: I don't even know you at all—how do I know I can trust you?

The Helper: You'll have to decide for yourself. But I can point you toward a path out of here. Would you like my help?

Me: Yes, okay. What do I need to do?

The Helper: I see the tracks of your car leading into this pothole. You've been trying to vault out of this rut in the same direction you entered it. But I think if you turn your wheels hard to the left, then slowly accelerate, your tires will actually follow the contours of the pothole out onto the flat surface again. Are you willing to give that a try?

Me: Well, it sounds very different from the strategies I was sure would help me, so it seems strange to me. But I'm going to take a big risk and trust you—I'll follow the path you've laid out and see what happens. Will you stay here close by while I give this a try?

The Helper: Of course—I'm not going anywhere until you're out of this pothole.

In schema therapy, the therapist offers the stuck person the kind of help best described as "limited reparenting." The goal is to "recognize, articulate, validate, and (to some extent) fulfill the needs of the patient." Once a trusting foundation has been established, the second "central pillar" of ST is what Jeffrey Young calls "empathic confrontation." This means the therapist, empathically and nonjudgmentally, confronts the patient about his or her maladaptive behaviors and thinking patterns, emphasizing their self-defeating impact. In other words, the goal is to find the toxic mold lurking under the surface, expose it to the light, then help the person to acknowledge its debilitating impact on his or her health. The therapist paints a picture of how the patient might have become stuck in the first place, then uses guided imagery to point toward a path out of the pothole. Sometimes the stuck person simply needs to "rehearse" the new narrative that will lead him or her to freedom before "walking into" that story. When the person takes steps to move out of the stuck place, the therapist is there to affirm, coach, and celebrate.

This pattern of intervention is more fluid and "everyday" than it sounds. Just today I (Rick) read a response from advice columnist Amy Dickinson that offers a perfect template for this surfacing/confronting strategy. A young father who hated his dad's "judgmental, critical, and mean" behavior toward his mother finds himself using the same "belittling language and angry tendencies" he'd vowed he would never adopt with his own family. He asks Dickinson: "Is this normal? Is there a way to quash this behavior? I want my kids and family to love me and always remember me for being a loving father, not an angry, belittling and critical jerk." Pay attention to the "path out of the pothole" that Dickinson offers this worried man:

> Dear Scared: You are not consigned to behave as your
> father did. You have every advantage—you have your

mother's good example, and (most important), you possess both awareness and the desire to change.

Stress will always bring out these very old scripts, but you can intentionally rewrite them, with your wife's help. Sit with her during a calm and private moment and talk about how you escalate these arguments. Always remember—when you're triggered, use "I" statements and never "you" statements. So—"YOU are a so-and-so" becomes "I feel angry/upset/out of control right now."

Remember that all-important "fight or flight" animal impulse? You should always choose "flight." Remove yourself. Cool down. Anchor to your best intentions. Unfortunately, many "I love yous" do not erase one "You're worthless." So—always, always apologize, and use specifics about what you are apologizing for. To your kids: "I'm so sorry I said that to you. I'm not being a good dad to you when I talk that way. My dad acted like that and I know how scary it is to be yelled at and called names. I'm going to remind myself to take a deep breath, count to ten, and stop myself from saying hurtful things that I don't mean."[4]

Here Dickinson "recognizes, articulates, and validates" the needs of "Scared," then offers gentle confrontation that spotlights the "self-defeating" impact of the man's maladaptive strategy for behaving differently than his abusive father (simply vowing he'll never do it). Instead, Dickinson offers a guided path out of this behavior pattern and invites "Scared" to follow it. She's found the mold, named it, exposed it to the light, and then invited the mold's "host" to rehearse a practical pathway out of the dark place.

Of course, schema therapy is just one among many strategies for identifying bugs in our narrative code. At Amen Clinics, we also use specific screeners for depression, anxiety, substance abuse, PTSD, and other bugs. We then make recommendations for therapies that match the individual (cognitive behavioral therapy, interpersonal therapy, dialectical behavioral therapy, eye movement desensitization and reprocessing [EMDR], and others). Trauma, depression, and anxiety also change how our brain functions, and they profoundly influence the conclusions we reach about our circumstances, our health, and our hope. This means some who struggle deeply with depression may not be aware how serious their situation is. And some, simply, are not as self-aware as others, or have not been educated on how depression can manifest itself, or refuse to accept what is happening to them because of our culture's stigmas about mental illness, or believe the religious myth that "Christians shouldn't be depressed—I just need more faith."

A healthy thought life, where toxic internal narratives are acknowledged and targeted in the light, is often planted and nurtured in the context of therapy. The therapist is the person who approaches our car that is stuck in a pothole, earns our trust, then helps us envision a way out of our stuckness. In cognitive behavioral therapy, the therapist:

- Works to help build awareness of the patient's lurking distortions
- Directly addresses the previously identified maladaptive core beliefs
- Surfaces intermediate beliefs (attitudes or rules we follow that typically apply across all situations in our life)
- Gently confronts automatic negative thoughts
- Intervenes to spotlight maladaptive behavioral patterns

The therapist addresses these challenges via cognitive interventions (new ways of thinking) or behavioral interventions (changing a behavior, which can have an upstream effect on thoughts and emotions). In

Western culture, we actually go to school to learn and adopt complex concepts, but we feel stigmatized for wanting to make a "learning investment" in our own brain health. Simply put, it's important to know and understand our story, and then tell it. Actionable knowledge (learning something about yourself and what to do to improve your situation) is empowering. It shifts the locus of control from outside circumstances to internal assets, which then shifts our frame of thinking. Remember, our default settings most often are infected by bugs, so we can't simply give ourselves over to default ways of thinking and doing. Put another way, our calling is to live intentionally. That means we routinely assess and reassess our thoughts, emotions, and behaviors. Then we consider whether or not they line up with our values and our faith in Jesus. Right now, as you're reading this book, you are making a courageous choice to live more intentionally.

Jesus as Therapist

As we've said, Jesus came to "debug" us—to bring into the light the "weaponized" narratives that have been implanted in our story, because we will live out the story our operating system is telling us about ourselves. We can see Jesus in all His debugging glory when He meets with the Apostle Peter just before He "ascends to the Father." Peter has committed a betrayal so monumental that it's difficult to see how he'll recover from it. He is lost and desperate and disoriented, caught in the web of his own toxic self-story. This is why, in John 21, he returns to the one thing (commercial fishing) that gives him a sense of "agency" and impact in his life. But this is a subtle form of avoidance, and it won't offer him the rescue he craves. And that's why Jesus invites him to share breakfast on the beach.

- For a second time, Peter encounters Jesus after a long night of frustration on his fishing boat—he's caught nothing, though he's a master fisherman. And Jesus calls out from the shore, telling Peter where to cast his nets. The catch is overwhelming—the "mystery man" on the beach is once again reminding Peter that he cannot simply find his own way out of the dark cave he's descended into. What we can't do, Jesus can do. And Peter, in his humility, dives over the side of the boat to accept Jesus's invitation to help.

- When Peter arrives on shore, Jesus has already built a fire and is cooking breakfast. He is inviting Peter to be served. And he asks Peter to add some of his catch to the meal. Here Jesus is reminding him, "I will help with what you need, but I want you to contribute, because I never move unilaterally to bring freedom when it's possible to partner." When the fish is done grilling, Jesus serves the entire party, a clear marker that He has upended forever the servant/Master relationship and replaced it with an intimate friend-to-friend relationship.

- With breakfast over, Jesus sets His sights on Peter's toxic interior narrative. Three times He asks him: "Do you love me?" His intention is to tap into His friend's core narrative by repeatedly poking at his wound. He does this until Peter becomes agitated: "Peter was hurt that Jesus asked the question a third time. He said, 'Lord, you know everything. You know that I love you'" (John 21:17). Peter's evident emotion is a signal that he is now aware of the toxic narrative that has been growing in the dark. Jesus has dragged it into the light—the first step in intervention.

- But Jesus isn't merely surfacing the "mold" in Peter's soul—each time, after Peter answers His "Do you love me?" question, He asks him to "feed my sheep." He is investing belief, responsibility, ownership, and trust in His friend—painting for him a vision of a path forward out of the dark. "I am counting on you, Peter, so here is the way out of your pothole."

- Finally, Jesus tells Peter that, contrary to the narrative that has grown in his darkness, he's going to die a hero. The passion that Peter repeatedly declared before his betrayal will be returned to him, whole and complete. And Jesus's "Follow me" is simply an invitation to begin living as He does—wholly.

We are complex people, and our problems and challenges require complex intervention. Only an artist can offer us a path to redemptive freedom that addresses our complexity but is also simple in its invitation— "Follow Me." But we have one more glaring need to address before we move (in Part Two) to our "menu of possibilities" for suicide-resistant, Jesus-inspired, "wholly living" practices. In the next chapter, we'll focus on strategies designed to address the bugs in our hardware—our biology and chemical makeup. These hardware bugs cannot be surfaced and removed the same way our software bugs can be. To address them, we'll need a wholly different kind of help.

CHAPTER 4

DEBUGGING OUR HARDWARE

How to Overcome Trauma, Brain Injury, Toxic Exposure, and Other Biological Barriers

When Jesus returns to His hometown, He encounters a paralyzed man lying on a mat. The man's friends have brought him to Jesus for healing (Matthew 9:1–8). When Jesus sees their faith, He's impressed and reassures the man: "Your sins are forgiven." The man is obviously in need of a physical healing—that's why his determined friends have brought him. But instead of addressing his biological captivity, Jesus first addresses his spiritual captivity. Sin is a death sentence over his soul, and Jesus is a life-giver. So he sets the man free by telling him "forgiven" is now his spiritual reality.

But this infuriates and offends the teachers of religious law, who mutter an angry question: "Does he think he is God?" And Jesus, studying how they're responding, lambastes their attitude as "evil." He then challenges these small-minded, self-righteous leaders to reconsider the way they've compartmentalized the physical and the emotional/spiritual aspects of our humanity. Our hardware (the man's paralysis) is no more important than our software (our mind, will, and emotions), so He addresses the most pressing need first. Then, almost as an afterthought, Jesus tells the man to "stand up, pick up your mat, and go home!" Translated into the context of our pursuit in this book, our software and hardware are equally important aspects of our human condition, and both need healing. Emotional and physical brokenness are equally paralyzing. And for those who are suffering a biological deficit of some kind—a bug in their hardware—merely following our guidelines for debugging software will not work. As Jesus demonstrated, our hardware and software work together to strengthen our response to dark or debilitating narratives, and each needs a different approach to healing and debugging.

In our work at Amen Clinics, we know there are often other factors contributing to people who struggle with depression, anxiety, and suicidal thinking that extend beyond negative schemas and cognitive disorders. An injured brain cannot wholly embrace and exercise the software strategies that lead to health any more than a car with a misfiring engine can transfer energy to the transmission and then the wheels. If you remain stuck in your pothole while others are giving you guidance on how to find your way out, urging you to power your way to freedom, it's deeply frustrating when your engine won't turn over. So, it's important to first identify potential brain injuries or alterations and then expand the treatment strategy beyond simply changing our self-narrative. We must move toward healing in our hardware/brain so that our software/soul has a functioning engine to empower it. This is vital, because it reinterprets our path out of the Valley of the Shadow of Death from one marked by stigma, shame, and guilt to something life-giving and healthy.

The problem is medical, not moral.

We're wrestling with an illness, not a failing.

That nagging inner voice—the one that insinuates that we don't change because we can't change—is a liar, not a truth-teller.

Two Vital Realizations

In the whole-person approach Jesus modeled, it's vital to embrace two important truths: An injury or deficit in our brain plays a major role in our psychological health, and we can do something to counteract that deficit and feel better. In Matthew 7, Jesus warns against building our life on a foundation of sand and urges us to build (instead) on a foundation of rock. Translated into the context of our soul's hardware, He's telling us that our biological foundation offers us either the solid footing we need to exercise our software solutions to challenges and traumas (truth that is acted upon), or the sandy, shifting surface that makes the tasks and responsibilities of everyday life exhausting (truth that can't be acted upon). We can push as hard as we want toward a healthy, holistic lifestyle, but if our feet are slipping out from underneath us all the time, we'll lose hope.

Truth #1: Our Hardware Is Contributing to the Way We're Feeling.

Beyond our negative schemas and cognitive distortions, bugs in our hardware can make us feel unwell. If you've had a head injury in your past, you're more likely to have a depressive episode. Even just one concussion can put you at higher risk; every person has a different trigger standard. Or if you have cardiovascular disease, it can impact blood flow to your brain, which then impacts how you feel. Or if you suffer with sleep apnea, that will impact the oxygenation to your brain, making it harder to use the skills we highlighted in Chapter Three. Likewise with diabetes and over-consumption of alcohol. Long-rutted patterns of thinking can also change the way your brain works—in other words, your software can plant a bug in your hardware. In addition to these prominent sources of hardware bugs, here's an extended sampler:

- Chemotherapy or radiation exposure

- Environmental toxins, such as mold
- Heavy metal exposure
- Carbon monoxide poisoning
- Anoxia or chronic hypoxia (deprivation of oxygen for several minutes from a heart attack, near-drowning, or even sleep apnea)
- Infections such as Lyme disease or herpes
- Hypothyroidism
- Severe anemia
- Autoimmune or inflammatory processes, such as allergies, infections, or lupus

Because hardware is a major contributor to the way we experience our reality, we might need biological interventions to give us the freedom and strength to pursue software solutions. For example, you might need medication to give you the added help you seek. But many people, especially people of faith, don't feel comfortable with that. Faith, in this distorted way of thinking, means we trust God alone to deal with our emotional/spiritual issues; medication is then a capitulation to our anemic Christian maturity. We have a hard time reconciling that the way we're feeling could be the result of a medical condition. And when we make this calculation, we're unwittingly practicing a form of everyday Gnosticism. The ancient Gnostic heretics believed that "matter" was evil and "spirit" was good. In essence, the material world—our physical and biological reality—was of little importance, because Gnosticism divorced the spiritual from the physical.

When it comes to our physical/biological health—for example, our relationship with exercise, nutrition, and fitness—those who follow Jesus are some of the most avid practitioners of Gnosticism. To wit: church members are more likely than those who don't attend a church to be more than 20 percent overweight.[1] I know this dynamic firsthand, because I (Rick) lived much of my adult life as a Gnostic Jesus-follower. I made the spiritual pursuit of Jesus my life's passion but allowed myself to get fifty pounds overweight and decidedly unfit. When I began to decompartmentalize my humanness and reject my Gnostic ways, I found the strength and determination to lose that weight, which in turn has deeply impacted my spiritual life.

Matthew McNutt is a longtime youth pastor and a former contestant on the weight-loss reality show *The Biggest Loser*. McNutt describes his own battle with practical Gnosticism:

> For years I didn't connect my spiritual health with my physical health. So while my heart and mouth claimed I belonged to Jesus, my 366-pound body proclaimed my lack of self-control, discipline, and respect for my body. Somewhere along the line I allowed the same Gnostic heresies that the Apostles fought thousands of years ago to invade my beliefs. In effect I lived a life that claimed my soul, not my physical body and biology, was my right priority. Like many of us, I took New Testament passages on our bodies being temples of the Holy Spirit and used them as warnings to teenagers against having sex or doing drugs, but I failed to see what these Scriptures had to do with my expanding waistline.[2]

Jesus said: "Love [Me] with all your heart, soul, mind, and strength." This is a holistic vision of love, and it opens our avenues of healing to a much wider range of interventions. At Amen Clinics, our SPECT scans help justify the way our patients are feeling. SPECT is a nuclear medicine technology that uses very small bursts of light called photons to study living tissue. The research on brain SPECT imaging is vast, with more than fourteen thousand scientific research articles listed on the National Institutes of Health website (https://pubmed.

ncbi.nlm.nih.gov). SPECT helps us asses how the brain is working by allowing us to study blood flow and activity, not simply the brain's structure (what standard MRI or CT procedures do). SPECT can help us answer three big questions about the functional activity in each area of the brain: 1) Is it healthy? 2) Is it underactive? 3) Is it overactive? In the standard practice of psychiatry, the brain's functional activity is often ignored—but we believe you can't treat what you can't see. And once we have a better handle on what sort of rescue is needed, we'll have a clearer picture of the way forward. Hard evidence from SPECT scans helps us expose and dismantle the false narrative that often restrains our patients from pursuing the healing God intends: "I'm just a failure in my faith. I'm depressed because I'm not a good enough Christian." To be blunt, this is how the devil lies to us. He is, as Jesus reminds us, "a liar and the father of lies" (John 8:44). And the lie he plants in us is the same lie insinuated by Gnosticism: your spiritual compartment isn't strong enough to compensate for your physical compartment, and you'll never be good enough to believe the way you need to believe.

It's arrogant to demand that God heal us in a particular way. If Jesus chooses to offer healing for our blindness by spitting in the dirt and smearing mud over our eyes, will we reject His "methodology"? Of course, He could've healed the blind man in John 9 with a word or a touch of His hand, but He invites the man to receive his healing in an indirect way instead. He smears His spit-mud on the man's face, then asks him to wash it off in the pool of Siloam, which will require effort and humility and vulnerability. It seems like a humiliating series of random prerequisites, but the "indirect means" of healing Jesus invites him to receive also describes the medical therapies that can help heal our bugged hardware.

If you prayed before you came to see me (Daniel) for counsel and treatment, then why wouldn't you be open to the indirect medical treatments I might recommend—alternate forms of spit-mud? All healing comes from God—and sometimes He uses the spit-mud of medicine as a tool. It's an act of faith to trust a doctor's healing regimen. It's not just the pill that brings healing; it's your taking that pill in the context of your faith in Jesus that completes that healing. In my experience, when patients resist potential pathways for healing, it's often driven by fear and a desire to control. Fear and control are not of God. Jesus is inviting us to approach Him with humility: "Why won't you humbly accept My grace however I choose to give it to you?"

A contemporary fable targets the faith-arrogance that keeps us from inviting the hardware debugging solutions Jesus is offering.

As floodwaters rose, a man found himself stuck on his rooftop. Desperate, he prayed for God's help. Soon a man in a rowboat passed by, shouting, "Jump in. I can save you." But the desperate man shouted back, "No, it's okay. I've asked God to save me." So the man in the rowboat shrugged his shoulders and rowed away. Then a powerboat cruised by, slowing to a stop in front of the man on the roof. The skipper shouted, "Jump in. I can save you." But again, the stranded man waved him off: "No thanks. I'm praying that God will save me. I have faith that He will." So the man in the powerboat shook his head and motored away. Then a helicopter appeared on the horizon, speeding toward the man on the roof until it hovered over him. The pilot shouted down, "Grab this rope and I will lift you to safety." And, of course, the stranded man shouted back up: "No thanks. I have faith that God is going to rescue me." So the pilot pulled the rope back up and headed off. Soon the water rose above the rooftop and the man who was holding out for God to rescue him drowned. In Heaven he approached God to complain about his unanswered prayer. "I had faith in you!" And, with a crooked smile, God

answered the man: "I sent you a rowboat and a powerboat
and a helicopter—what more did you want?"

The rowboat/powerboat/helicopter rescue Jesus is offering must
be invited and accepted; He won't force us into healing. And because
He's a guide, not a genie, He will extend His hand, not snap His fingers. That means we humbly seek and humbly receive our healing on
His terms, not ours. To bow before Him means to give way to Him—
as John the Baptist proclaimed, "He must become greater and greater,
and I must become less and less" (John 3:30). He does not mean that
his identity or agency is obliterated; he means that he (the lesser) wor-
ships the Greater by giving way to Him. It's an act of trust and love
and dependence and honor.

Truth #2: We Can Do Something to Debug Our Hardware.

Because our biology—our hardware—seems fixed and immovable,
hope for debugging it can seem improbable. But it is possible, even
probable, that we can significantly impact the effects and influence of
our hardware bugs. We have many intervention options.

What We Can Do without the Help of Others

After Jesus smears mud on the blind man's eyes, He tells him to
find the Pool of Siloam and wash in it. Jesus does something, but
then the blind man does something that he's been told to do, and
Jesus does not hold his hand and walk him to the Pool of Siloam.
Once we know what is right and good to do, Jesus expects us to follow through on what we know. A few examples will help us to
understand what this looks like, then we'll explore them in greater
depth and detail in Part Two.

Diet and exercise. Of course, what we eat and how we take care
of our body impacts our quality of life. But food and fitness also have

a direct impact on our brain health, and therefore our biology. For example, we can cut back on sugar—excess glucose impairs both our cognitive skills and our self-control. And we can avoid a sedentary lifestyle by exercising five times a week for twenty minutes—physical inactivity is linked to thinning in regions of the brain that are critical to memory formation. In our diet, we can eat more avocados, nuts, seeds, spinach, sweet potatoes, broccoli, beets, celery, garlic, chickpeas, and mushrooms—all of them proven to boost brain health. Likewise, we can limit salt, alcohol, caffeine (one serving a day), fruit juices, and sodas. Instead, we can drink at least five glasses of water a day.

Follow the advice of professionals. If a doctor, psychologist, nutritionist, fitness expert, or coach recommends a strategy to boost your brain health, follow through. That means taking your blood pressure medicine and your vitamins and your nutritional supplements. Don't ignore or delay treating health problems such as hypertension, sleep apnea, low testosterone, thyroid dysfunction, and drug or alcohol abuse. Stay consistent with any medications you've been prescribed. Sleep seven or eight hours a night. And stop ingesting nicotine or smoking marijuana.

Pursue natural brain-health influencers. Take a walk in nature—research shows this can decrease the activity in areas of the brain that are associated with mental illness. Consider natural dietary supplements that increase blood flow in the brain—for example, ginkgo biloba, Omega-3 fatty acids found in fish oil, green tea catechins, and resveratrol, the plant compound found in red wine. Also, Vitamin E is an antioxidant and helps with brain health by reducing oxidative stress.

What We Need Help to Do

When Jesus intervenes with "the woman caught in adultery" (John 8:1–11), He is helping someone who no longer has the freedom or the means to help herself. If a rescuer does not intervene in her story to help, she's going to die. She does not have agency over her rescue. And when the help we need is outside our expertise or capability, or we have no fight left in us, then we need others to fight for us. For example, if you or someone you know is acutely suicidal, you (or your friend) will need outside assistance to implement the ideas in this book. Again, a few examples will point to the way forward, and we'll take a deeper dive in Part Two.

Finding and stopping the toxin or infection that is assaulting your hardware. It's well-known that high mercury or lead or PCB levels in our groundwater can permanently impact brain health. The chronic effects of mold exposure and Lyme disease can also compromise the health of a susceptible brain. If you suspect exposure to these toxins, get tested and treated by medical professionals.

Treating potential causes of inflammation, such as the "standard American diet," food allergies, or lupus. At a base level, when we get sick, some germs can attack the brain and cause swelling that leads to injury—that's called encephalitis, or meningitis, when the lining of the brain becomes inflamed. Neuro-oncologist Dr. Santosh Kesari says, "Inflammation in the brain can be due to a variety of reasons, including toxins in the body like tobacco or cocaine, diabetes, hypertension, infections, trauma, aging, diet, and stress."[3] Lupus and other inflammatory conditions can inflame the blood vessels in the brain. Food allergies can have a far-reaching impact on brain functioning, producing anxiety, agitation, confusion, depression, palpitations, sweating, and mental slowness or "brain fog." And while the standard American diet sounds innocuous, regular high intake of red meat, processed meat, prepackaged foods, butter, candy and other sweets, fried foods, conventionally raised animal products, high-fat dairy products, eggs, refined grains, potatoes, corn, high-fructose corn syrup, and high-sugar drinks can altogether produce higher levels of inflammation in your body. That— combined with sporadic and low intake of brain-healthy foods such as fruits, vegetables, whole grains, grass-fed animal products, fish, nuts, and seeds—can create a perfect storm that undermines our ability to push back against encroaching psychological darkness. **Eliminating allergens.** An allergy is more than a seasonal sneezing fit; it's a chronic inflammatory disease that affects one out of five people in the Western world. New research shows that chronic allergic reactions lead to increased inflammation in the brain, influencing the onset of diseases such as Alzheimer's. See an allergist and get tested— it's relatively easy, and it could change your life by giving you the insight you need to avoid allergic "triggers."

Treating underlying medical issues. Chronic illnesses carry some of the same risks for depression and suicide as the two "classic" risk factors—a family history of depression and a family member who has taken his or her own life. We know degenerative conditions such as Parkinson's disease and strokes cause changes in the brain that can lead to depression. And the anxiety and stress that a chronic illness brings on can also trigger suicidal ideation. Depression is common among people who have chronic illnesses such as cancer, coronary heart disease, diabetes, epilepsy, multiple sclerosis, Alzheimer's, HIV/AIDS, lupus, and rheumatoid arthritis. Also, if we can boost our hormonal function (treating low testosterone, hypothyroidism, and so on), we can also improve our mood, motivation, energy, and cognitive functioning. When we lessen the impact of a chronic condition, the brain can recover its ability to better regulate its interior narrative.

Rehabilitate your brain. When we suffer a physical injury, we need a rehabilitation program to return to health. And the same is true for brain injuries or deficits. At Amen Clinics, our brain-rehabilitation strategies include:

- Avoiding anything that further harms the brain
- Engaging in regular brain-healthy habits (improved nutrition, exercise, new learning, and so on)

- Neurofeedback—a type of biofeedback that uses real-time displays of brain electrical activity (usually through EEG monitoring) to teach patients to self-regulate their brain function
- Hyperbaric oxygen therapy—HBOT can boost production of stem cells that promote healing
- Targeted nutraceuticals and medications

A Fitness Model for the Brain

We're all born with a certain level of "brain reserve"—the cognitive fuel tank that helps us power through the potholes in our road and gives us the horsepower to move into and out of ruts. Just as our muscle tone deteriorates as we get older, our brain's "muscle power" also weakens. Our lifestyle, health habits, and brain-engaging activities all contribute to brain fitness. And these factors either grow or diminish our brain reserve. Dr. Daniel Amen, my longtime colleague and founder of Amen Clinics, says: "In general, the more brain reserve you have, the more resilient you are and the better your brain can handle the aging process to keep 'mental health' disorders at bay.... A growing body of science is showing that even before you were conceived, your parents' lifestyle habits were laying the foundation for your overall wellbeing and physical and mental health."[4]

From the moment our brain begins developing in our mother's womb, all of us have a "bank" of brain reserve. But if your mom was exposed to cigarette smoke or overindulged in alcohol or ate a high-fat diet or was always stressed about her health or finances, those factors depleted the reserve in your "brain bank." But if your mom avoided cigarette smoke and ate a low-fat, plant-based diet and used dietary supplements and handled the stress in her life with good humor, all of

those factors added to your "brain bank." And these deposits and
withdrawals from your bank will continue the rest of your life.

Deposits	Withdrawals
• Stable Home	• Chronic Stress
• Healthy Diet	• Domestic Abuse
• Little Exposure to Contact Sports	• Traumatic Brain Injury
• Non-Smoker	• Marijuana Use
• Reduce Inflammation in Your Body	• Junk Food Diet
• Many Educational Opportunities	• Limited Educational Opportunities

This, of course, is a good news/bad news truth—we can debug our
hardware and work to lessen the impact of our biological deficits, and
we can also make things worse than they need to be. The old maxim
"God helps those who help themselves" is a form of Phariseeism in its
extreme—a subtle way to wrest control away from God. But there is
a seed of truth in it. Jesus won't do for us what He can do with us. To
the extent we are available and capable, it would be disrespectful of
Jesus to overrule our own participation in our healing. We've been
invited into intimate friendship with Him, not a master-slave relationship: "I no longer call you slaves, because a master doesn't confide in
his slaves. Now you are my friends, since I have told you everything
the Father told me" (John 15:15). Jesus invites us to partner with Him

by intentionally working to improve our brain fitness, making deposits into our brain reserve as a critical part of our healing.

In Part Two, we'll explore a wide range of ideas and strategies that target both our software and hardware health—all of them connected to the truths and behavior patterns modeled by Jesus.

OUT OF THE VALLEY

David wrote his most famous worship song, Psalm 23, after he'd been crowned king—but the foundation for it was laid during his formative years, when he was serving his family's "small business" as a shepherd. From an early age, he protected and provided for his father's sheep and goats. We know from his own history-giving that when "a lion or a bear [came] to steal a lamb from the flock," he would "go after it with a club and rescue the lamb from its mouth." And if an animal attacked him, he would "catch it by the jaw and club it to death." It's in that close, personal familiarity with the hard realities of shepherding that he wrote these words:

> *The Lord is my shepherd;*
> *I have all that I need.*
> *He lets me rest in green meadows;*
> *he leads me beside peaceful streams.*
> *He renews my strength.*
> *He guides me along right paths,*

bringing honor to his name.
Even when I walk
through the darkest valley,
I will not be afraid,
for you are close beside me.
Your rod and your staff
protect and comfort me.

For David, "good shepherding" meant risking your life for your sheep, facing danger on their behalf, and caring for their needs. Jesus embraced this same standard for good shepherding:

- A compassionate determination to care for the needy. When He traveled around the region surrounding His hometown of Nazareth, Jesus studied the crowds that quickly grew up around Him: "When he saw the crowds, he had compassion on them because they were confused and helpless, like sheep without a shepherd" (Matthew 9:36).
- A heart for knowing, and being known by, those He serves. After Jesus heals the man born blind in John 9, sparking indignation and fury among the offended religious leaders, He bluntly (and metaphorically) describes His heart toward those in need: "I tell you the truth, anyone who sneaks over the wall of a sheepfold, rather than going through the gate, must surely be a thief and a robber! But the one who enters through the gate is the shepherd of the sheep. The gatekeeper opens the gate for him, and the sheep recognize his voice and come to him. He calls his own sheep by name and leads them out" (John 10:1–3).

- A passionate desire to offer the needy an abundant life. Jesus frames His purpose in simple terms. He wants to bring freedom to our captivity in life, so we can experience true joy: "Those who come in through me will be saved. They will come and go freely and will find good pastures. The thief's purpose is to steal and kill and destroy. My purpose is to give them a rich and satisfying life" (John 10:9–10).
- An unwavering commitment to risk everything on our behalf. Like David before him, Jesus is no ordinary shepherd; he's a ferocious provider and protector who will never back down from a threat: "I am the good shepherd. The good shepherd sacrifices his life for the sheep. A hired hand will run when he sees a wolf coming. He will abandon the sheep because they don't belong to him and he isn't their shepherd. And so the wolf attacks them and scatters the flock. The hired hand runs away because he's working only for the money and doesn't really care about the sheep" (John 10:11–13).

We, like David, can find our way out of the Valley of the Shadow of Death if we will follow the Good Shepherd who promises to be "close beside" us. The Jesus who will not run when He sees a wolf coming at us, who will work all the time to give us a "rich and satisfying life," and who will guide us with the blessing of our permission instead of forcing us to do what He wants ("entering through the gate" rather than "sneaking over the wall" like a thief) invites us to choose from a deep and wide storehouse of ideas, strategies, and practices that will bring us out of the valley and into the light.

CHAPTER 5

ESCAPING THROUGH THE SIDE DOOR

Why Frontal Approaches to Defusing Our Destructive Narratives Rarely Work and How "Oblique" Strategies Lead to Freedom

I (Rick) first noticed something had changed in Maria when she stopped sharing and responding to questions in the church ministry my wife and I once led several years ago. She'd always been deep, thoughtful, and eager to share—a remarkably insightful, thoroughly enjoyable young woman. But then she left for a job out of state, and something exploded in her soul.

On the on-ramp to her adult life, she'd hit an emotional roadside bomb. She was surrounded by others who were making new connections and relishing new freedoms, but she felt isolated, disoriented, and hopeless. Her confidence, so easy and relaxed before, disappeared like a vapor. On a vacation trip back to our town, she returned to see us at the ministry, but never opened her mouth. She smiled and listened and nodded her head, but the effort required to keep all of that up was obvious. A longtime friend who'd reconnected with her, and who also was involved in the ministry, looked at me and complained bluntly: "I wish she'd stop apologizing all the time for everything."

As soon as we closed in prayer, my wife, Bev, moved to the empty seat next to Maria and put an arm around her, whispering in her ear: "Sweetheart, I see you withering on the vine." And then the sobs welled up from her core, and Maria couldn't stop shaking. More than thirty minutes later, she was still sitting crumpled in her seat, cradled in Bev's arms, weeping. Clearly, we were experiencing the devastating consequences of a great trauma. But, we knew, nothing really terrible—in the conventional way we define trauma—had happened to her. She'd left home for a promising start to her career, far from home and old friends. That qualifies as a challenging rite of passage, but not often a trauma. Even so, the evidence of destructive impact was undeniable. She'd lost herself—the same sensation we feel when we wade into the ocean until our feet leave the sand and we're floating, untethered and ungrounded.

Bev's first attempts to help Maria were, predictably, a frontal assault against the obvious sources of her lostness:

> I started to say things I believed about her situation. I told her the job environment she'd chosen was not helping her, that she was obviously not thriving, and that I wanted to see her find a new job where she could be herself. For whatever reason, [her current position] wasn't the place for that. I told her that I knew her family thought she should persevere in this job, but I believed she'd already tried long enough to make it work. I told her I was not trying to tell her what to do, but that I believed in her. She was crying through all of this, apologizing for everything. She tried to say some things to me, but she couldn't stop crying long enough to do it. Finally, she was able to tell me that she was frightened by the prospect of disappointing everyone in her life if she left her job and returned home.

Maria was at war with herself.

- She didn't understand why things had turned out the way they had.
- She didn't understand why she was not free to be herself.
- She didn't understand how new career paths had worked out for her friends but not for her.
- She didn't understand why she was so bound up and why trying harder didn't help.
- And she didn't understand why her logical, determined efforts to refute the lies she was embracing about herself ("I'm flawed and unworthy and unenjoyable and not enough") had failed so miserably.

Maria was trying as hard as she could to frontally engage and defeat a destructive threat to her soul, but those head-on efforts had no impact. Bev doubled down by repeating the same default truths that Maria had already tried to embrace, but to no avail. Whatever was happening to her, talking her way out of it wasn't going to work. She'd been taken captive by a destructive narrative that was operating like a terrorist in her life. Likely, that narrative had been operating under the radar in her life for a long time, and the circumstances surrounding her transition into a new job triggered it into activity. This sort of terrorist cannot be overpowered by the frontal assault of sheer willpower or nurturing, compassionate words. Maria couldn't be herself because she'd lost herself. She couldn't connect with her old friends because she felt like a shell of a person; she believed she had nothing inside her that others could connect to. It was, of course, confusing for her friends, but she was afraid they'd discover she had nothing left inside. She couldn't bear to be around them because it was too exhausting to uphold a façade of normalcy.

In the face of a destructive narrative that has become embedded in our soul, the conventional frontal solutions we throw at the problem—repeated attempts to mirror back the truth, impassioned pep talks, armchair psychoanalysis, and even some pharmaceutical attempts to correct a chemical imbalance in the brain—have marginal lasting impact. The cancer in our soul that triggers our descent into the Valley of the Shadow of Death has been shrewdly planted, and it must be shrewdly uprooted.

The Oblique Approach to Fighting Back

A destructive narrative is designed to destroy. That might seem like an obvious truth, but we don't often recognize the intent behind the interior lies we entertain. The twisted stories we tell about ourselves have the same impact as a psychopath slipping a little arsenic into our breakfast cereal every day, then watching with enjoyment as we slowly die an agonizing (and oblivious) death. Abuse and trauma and wounding can carry with them a narrative designed to destroy. We all hunger for a "truth" that completes the jigsaw puzzle of our life, even if that truth is actually a lie. We must heed the Apostle Peter's warning: "Stay alert! Watch out for your great enemy, the devil. He prowls around like a roaring lion, looking for someone to devour" (1 Peter 5:8). A prowling lion has no concern for the gazelle's feelings; he's a predator, and he's looking for food. Jesus reminds us that we have nothing to fear from those who can "merely" kill our body. Instead, we should fear "only God, who can destroy both soul and body in hell" (Matthew 10:28).

The mind of the prowling lion has embraced this reality. Killing the body might do damage, but it won't destroy. He intends to destroy what is eternal—namely, our God-given identity. The obliteration of our soul—our intrinsic identity—is the wellspring of murder. And weaponizing our interior narrative is the most effective and undetectable method to use.

Against this destructive intent, frontal defenses have a minimal effect and are short-lived. Only oblique leverage has the power to surface, dislodge, and eradicate the narrative cancer that is consuming our soul.

Oblique means "non-direct"—it's an angle of approach that comes from the side, not from the front. A vaccine is a classic "oblique" strategy for fighting disease—training the immune system to fight a viral or bacterial invader by introducing an "antibody kickstarter" before the real attacker arrives. When an "antigen," the foreign invader, attacks the body, immune cells called lymphocytes respond by producing protein antibodies. These antibodies fight the disease process. But the first time the body faces a particular invader, it can take several days to ramp up an antibody response. For some dangerous antigens (COVID-19, measles, or whooping cough, for example), a few days is too long. The infection, for those who are susceptible, can spread and kill the person before the immune system can fight back. The frontal assault against the invader is too little, too late. But the sideways approach, tricking the immune system into fight mode before the fight begins, saves lives.

Let's consider the way we protect our destructive narratives by using a common plot device from the old TV show *Star Trek* as a metaphor. Let's say a threatening alien ship is approaching the *Enterprise*. Captain Kirk sees the threat and orders his ship's engineer, Scotty, to redirect all power to the front shields to ward off a direct attack.

"Full power to the shields, Mr. Scott!" Kirk orders.

"Giving 'em all we got!" Scotty cries.

Now, if the attack is directed at those front shields, the ship is likely to survive the assault. But if the aliens present a frontal attack simply to distract Captain Kirk, while sending a second ship to secretly approach the *Enterprise* from the side, where the shields are completely down, victory is theirs. The way to get past the fortified defenses of a destructive narrative is to confront it sideways.

Our killer narratives, like deadly viruses, have a strong survival instinct and are well-prepared for frontal attacks against them. Our narratives have heard all the conventional push-back strategies and have already mounted their own immune response to them, but a sideways approach fueled by kindness might actually take them off guard. We thank the narratives that have turned destructive in our life for helping us to survive our trauma initially, then release them from service.

The stories we tell ourselves have remarkable staying power. This is why we so often fail to convince people (like Maria) who've embraced and ingested lying narratives about themselves to accept and adopt the truth instead. The destructive narratives we're trying so hard to dislodge from their souls use a defense strategy that unconsciously transfers all of their protective energies to their "front shields." People who are "stuck in a moment" may well be aware of the destructive power of their interior narratives, and even hate the impact they have on their life, but the direct approaches others use to defeat them hardly ever succeed. If we hope to eradicate the self-talking lies that are destroying people we care about, we will have to confront them from the side, where the "shields are down." But we rarely do this, because "sideways" strategies seem confusing, counterintuitive, and risky. Therefore, it's crucial to understand the power of "sideways" leverage in a diversity of contexts so we can wield its powerful impact when we engage our well-defended narratives (and those of others). For example:

Jesus does not urge us to simply try harder in our efforts to "keep the Law." He tells us we have no hope of attaining righteousness by strength of will (a frontal approach He debunks in Matthew 5:20).

Instead, He offers an oblique solution to our problem. He will exchange His righteousness for the "filthy rags" of our willful efforts to maintain our goodness, giving us what we could not earn by trying harder. Jazz is an oblique art form, in contrast to classical music, which takes a linear approach. The greatest distinction between the two hinges on improvisation—simply, jazz musicians learn the chord changes in a song, along with the melody, but then play loose improvisations that enter and exit from the "sides" of that melody. Often, these side excursions wander so far off the beaten path that the melody is lost altogether, returning only near the end of the song. In classical music, these oblique excursions would destroy the structure and are impossible to organize as planned notes on a sheet of music.

Translating the differences between oblique forms of music (jazz) and frontal/linear forms of music (classical) into the broader language of our life, British economist John Kay writes: "The process in which well-defined and prioritized objectives are broken down into specific states and actions whose progress can be monitored and measured [like following notes on a page in classical music] is not the reality of how people find fulfillment in their lives, create great art, establish great societies or build good businesses."[1] Another way of saying this is that great relationships have a "jazz" feel to them— they're fueled by improvisational, sideways surprises that open up our vulnerability, making it possible for us to love with our whole heart. But poor relationships—a master/slave relationship (or abuser/ victim), for example—operate on a system of predetermined "notes" and specifically eradicate improvisations as a threat to the stability of the relationship.

The examples of principle-based "frontal" teaching in Jesus's ministry are few (the Sermon on the Mount in Matthew 5–7, for example), while the examples of oblique teaching are many (the fifty-five parables He told, and the many debates He engaged in with His disciples and the Pharisees, not to mention the times He asked his disciples to walk on water or cast out demons or catch fish that had coins in their mouths). Over and over, Jesus prodded people to approach problems and challenges obliquely. This is why He so often prefaced His teaching by saying, "You have heard it said..." (the frontal/conventional/traditional approach to truth), followed by, "But I say..." (an oblique/Kingdom-of-God approach to truth). For example, He first references a commonly accepted frontal truth ("You have heard it said that you shall love your neighbor and hate your enemy") but follows it with an oblique push-back approach ("But I say to you, love your enemies and pray for those who persecute you..."). Hatred for your enemies will only fuel their hatred of you. Loving your enemies will plant in them the seeds of redemption. The oblique approach conquers when the frontal approach cannot deliver enough force to influence a change. This is why the oblique approach of thanking your negative schemas for their temporary help in your life, admitting their destructive influence now, then releasing them forever, has a better chance of freeing you from their captivity than railing against them and vowing to change.

Sideways Strategies for Confronting Destructive Narratives

Since the lie-viruses that infect us (most often from when we are children) outlive their practical survival purpose as we move into adulthood, they will kill us if they're allowed to continue to grow. So, what will eradicate these once-useful, but now-toxic narratives? These oblique strategies are starting points:

1. First, we identify and admit our toxic narratives—then summon the courage to tell others about them.

If we're trying to fight off a virus, we already know the conventional strategies: wash our hands often and thoroughly, cover our coughs and sneezes, social-distance from others, get plenty of sleep, make sure we don't rub our eyes or mouth after we've touched our nose, eat lots of fruits and vegetables, take Vitamin C, use wipes or hand sanitizer, and so on. But once the virus finds a way into our body, it's tough to kill—antibiotics don't always work, and vaccines will protect us only against certain strains. However, as we explored in Chapter Three, there is a defense against viruses that seems counter-intuitive at first: light can be used to kill them.

Researchers at Arizona State University and Johns Hopkins University discovered that strong blasts of light from a low-power laser can eradicate viruses. The laser, which shines for only one hundred femtoseconds, causes the virus's capsid (the outer shell) to vibrate and break apart, deactivating it.[2] Jesus understands this dynamic because He engineered it from the beginning of all things: "Everything that is hidden will eventually be brought into the open, and every secret will be brought to light" (Mark 4:22). Dragging our destructive lies that thrive in darkness into the light is the first sideways step toward releasing what has us in its grip, thus "vibrating and breaking apart" the shell of our "I'm okay, I'm okay, I'm okay" façade.

Jesus's encounter with the "woman with an issue of blood" (Luke 8:40–48) is a study in sideways, redemptive leverage. The woman is ostracized from society because her condition makes her "unclean"; she is desperate for healing, and her soul has been formed by shame. Remarkably, her desperation propels her toward a shocking risk: She will attempt to get close enough to the Rabbi to touch the hem of His garment, even though she is forbidden to approach Him. And though she is instantly healed, she quickly tries to escape without detection. But Jesus does not want her to disappear into the shadows.

First, He turns, scanning the crowd, searching the faces, and then proclaims: "Someone deliberately touched me, for I felt healing power go out from me." When the woman realizes that she cannot stay hidden, she begins to tremble and falls to her knees in front of Him (her "shell" is breaking apart). The whole crowd hears her explain why she's touched Him (she's exposing the seeds of her destructive narrative to others) and that she's been immediately healed. "Daughter," He says to her, "your faith has made you well. Go in peace."

Her physical condition represents a surface captivity, but shame is the weed that has roots so deep nothing will pull them up. She intends to stay hidden, protecting that weed from discovery. But Jesus intends to expose her shame to the light—to draw it out the same way we slowly, gently pull up a weed that has been allowed to grow for too long in our garden. He insists that the woman publicly own her healing—and "the whole crowd heard her explain why she had touched him...." Shame that is perpetuated by the crowd must be uprooted in the middle of the crowd. It must be proclaimed and embraced in the light, not buried in the darkness. And when the woman admits what she had intended to hide, Jesus tenderly and intimately renames her "daughter." And He invites her to lay down the weapons she has used to survive in the war of shame that has raged inside her and enter a new season of peace.

I (Rick) have a friend who, years ago, hid an eating disorder from his friends and family. As time passed, his dysfunctional and dangerous relationship with food (fueled by a destructive narrative that tied his need for acceptance to his weight) grew deeper roots in his soul. He was headed toward physical and psychological destruction. That is, until his wife accidentally discovered his purging addiction. At first, my friend promised he'd never purge again (a frontal effort at willing himself to stop), and his wife took him at his word. And he did fine for awhile—until he didn't. When his wife learned that he'd "gone off the wagon," she threatened to tell his coworkers and his friends the ugly truth. This threat—an oblique strategy that focused on his fear of exposure, not the mechanics of my friend's addiction—did the trick. My friend stopped the pattern of his eating disorder cold turkey— something that's almost impossible to do using conventional (frontal) strategies. When an eating-disorder professional asked my friend how he managed such an impossible feat, he said his fear of exposure was stronger than his need to purge. This threat of exposure paved the way for my friend to identify and admit the destructive narrative fueling his hidden behavior, then take his first steps into the light. It's a sideways rescue—light penetrating the darkness.

When my future wife returned from a year overseas as a missionary, she was a faint carbon copy of the Bev I had known for years. Something devastating had happened to her during the time she was helping launch an evangelism training ministry on a remote Mediterranean island. Once home again, she isolated herself from others, had a hard time making eye contact with anyone, and was so unsure of herself that she couldn't decide which pair of shoes to wear. She was stuck in a psychological rut, spinning her wheels, and descending into the Valley of the Shadow of Death. A friend of mine recommended a good counselor, and I passed on the contact information to Bev. After the counselor unearthed the details of her time on the island, she said: "Okay, you've been brainwashed. You've given other people the right and access to define you. And that's why you can't make small or big decisions."

The counselor explained what had happened to Bev—she had accepted and then ingested a host of destructive narratives about herself, all of them resonant with the foundational narratives of her damaging past—then helped her to first acknowledge, then diffuse, the impact of these rooted beliefs. She did this by exposing the "non-normal" narratives about herself she'd been coerced to accept, comparing the extreme beliefs propagated by her missionary leaders to the "conventional practices" of the Christian life. The counselor asked Bev to wrestle with a glaring-light question: "Why did you let this happen to you when others didn't?" The leaders in charge of the ministry on the island had a strong authoritarian message about "the right way" to live your Christian life. Others just blew off some of the more extreme things they said, but Bev did not. "I was incapable of doing that," she says. "I was a sponge, relative to my identity." Once these dark truths about her internal narrative were dragged into the light, they were exposed as starkly inconsistent with the "fearfully and wonderfully made" reality of her God-given identity. And her counselor patiently and persistently helped her to grasp the destructive intent of her threatening narratives by labeling their insidious form: "brainwashing."

Once Bev understood the dynamics of how brainwashing works, and why some people are vulnerable to it while others are not, she could engage her own determination to reject the subtly destructive lies she'd been embracing. If her counselor had tried, instead, to convince her to accept the truth about herself, Bev's "front shields" would have deflected that assault. But the sideways approach—helping her understand the mechanics of brainwashing and exposing the fallacies of her authoritarian leaders' beliefs—allowed her to slowly reclaim her own identity.

2. Second, we compare the "truth" our lies are insinuating with the truth of what Jesus says and does.

You've probably heard that U.S. Secret Service agents, who are charged with stopping the circulation of counterfeit money in addition to other duties, spend their time and attention studying actual bills, not counterfeit ones. In *Reckless Faith*, author John MacArthur writes: "Federal agents don't learn to spot counterfeit money by studying the counterfeits. They study genuine bills until they master the look of the real thing. Then when they see the bogus money they recognize it."[3]

I (Rick) asked a close friend who'd been sexually abused as a young boy about what helped him to face and overcome the destructive narratives that emerged from his trauma. "I began to be suspicious of the narrative," he says. "I read things in Scripture that didn't jibe with my narrative. If Jesus says I'm a beloved son and brother, but I feel completely unjustified in receiving love, then those two things don't mesh. I began asking God to tell me the truth about myself." Essentially, he focused all his time and attention on the "genuine bills" revealed in Scripture, not the plausible lies that were dragging him underwater.

My friend decided to try something radical—he found and recorded "truth about my identity" Scripture passages, then put ear buds in as he went to bed and fell into a deep sleep listening to these truths every night. "Over time I began to embrace the new narrative, and believe it," he says. "It got past my mental defenses because I circumvented my normal (waking) defense mechanisms. I used the side door."

Maria, our young friend who is still struggling to reclaim her stolen identity, first tried to confront her dire situation with hyper-spirituality. She told herself that the more spiritual she could be, the more likely it would be that she could beat the lies that had overtaken her narrative. But we need a receptivity to the kindness of Jesus, not frontal-attack religious formulas, to overshadow and contest our killer beliefs. The late singer-songwriter John Prine opens his song "Boundless Love" with these lyrics:

> I woke up this morning to a garbage truck.
> Looks like this ol' horseshoe's done run outta luck.
> If I came home, would you let me in?
> Fry me some pork chops and forgive my sin?[4]

Here Prine is exposing his interior life to the light, and a garbage truck emerges from the shadows. He does not try to argue his way out of what the light has revealed; he simply requests permission to come home again. He is the "Prodigal Son" who is not asking for a restoration of his status as an heir, but is simply determined to come home again, where he will throw himself on the mercy of his father's kindness. Religious formulas—"If I say the right words, in the right order, in the right tone of voice, and do all of the right things, I'll get the outcome I want"—have no power against our destructive narratives and can actually make them worse.

The sideways leverage of "Why?" can help us establish a "comparison pattern" when we confront our destructive narratives. When we use "Why?" questions to repeatedly pursue the foundations of the lies we tell ourselves, while simultaneously pursuing the foundations of truth as revealed and modeled by Jesus, we produce a stark comparison that offers us a pathway out of our canyon of despair. Here's an example of what I mean:

Bev came home on a furlough from the missionary field convinced, as her leaders had urged her to embrace, that an all-in commitment to Jesus would require her to give up not just her home in America, but her identity as an American. To be fully committed, they told her, she'd need to toss out that old identity and replace it with a new identity as an island-native for the rest of her life. She believed she must deny "the truth of her being" so that Jesus could have every part of her. Here is how her counselor's "Why?" sideways assault on that destructive narrative pointed her toward a path out of the darkness.

> Counselor: "But why would Jesus ask you to turn your back on your history and heritage to follow Him?"
> Bev: "Because He wants us to give everything to Him, even our nationality."
> Counselor: "But why would Jesus need you to give up your cultural identity? Do you see evidence of Him doing that with anyone else, ever?"
> Bev: "Well, I can't think of an example right now..."
> Counselor: "So why would your leaders on the island ask you to do something so radical, when Jesus never asked the pagan 'untouchables' He healed to reject their cultural identity in order to follow Him?"
> Bev: "I guess I don't know why they insisted on this 'island identity' thing with me."

Here, the foundations of the killer lie are starting to "vibrate and break apart," and her curiosity and determination are beginning to resurface. Yes, God may invite us to sacrifice many things to live out our calling, but He will not ask us to prove our commitment by killing our soul. To find our way out of our own Grand Canyons of despair, and help others to do the same, we use the oblique leverage of "Why?" questions as guides. And we ask "Why?" over and over and over, until we start to pull down the pillars that are holding up our destructive narratives.

3. **Third, we invite others to offer us a "truth sonar" for our soul.** My friend who experienced childhood sexual abuse says, "I decided to pay attention to the fruit my interior narrative was producing in my life. I noticed that certain trains of thought were producing horrible fruit. That made me suspicious of what I was internally professing. The voice I heard inside was telling me, over and over: 'You are not worth anyone's time.' I really thought that voice was telling the truth, but it produced in me a kind of darkness, and an unwillingness to be vulnerable." What helped him in this "sonar" assessment was a counterintuitive weapon—comparison. "I became conscious of my destructive narratives through comparison—I had friends who were much more carefree than me. So why was I different?"

Sonar uses the aural dynamics of an echo to find and describe a hidden object. Animals, people, and machines make noises, emitting sound waves into their environment. Those waves bounce off objects, and some of them reflect back to the object that made the noise. It's those reflected sound waves that we hear when our voice echoes back to us in a canyon. Whales and bats use reflected waves to locate distant objects and "describe" their shape and movement. The range of low-frequency sonar is remarkable. Dolphins and whales can tell the difference between objects as small as a BB pellet from fifty feet away, and they use sonar much more than sight to find their food, families, and direction.[5]

The point is that it's almost impossible for us to escape our destructive narratives outside of a knowing community. Some, like my pastor friend with the eating disorder, try to contain the nuclear impact of their destructive thinking by "capping" it inside their soul. My abuse-survivor friend had a wise counselor who challenged him out of his isolation: "Someone has to pay for your sin," she told him, "and that's the role of community. The community has to pay the price for it, so you can experience grace being offered to you." It's counterintuitive to expose something hurtful about us to others we care about, but it's the experience of grace, offered by the midwives of grace who are our friends and family, that upsets the permanence of our embedded lies.

Finally, the longing to experience the freedom others have will often surface poison in us. When I (Rick) asked my wife to consider what has been most helpful to her as she emerges from the shadow of her killer narratives, she said: "You have modeled a different kind of relationship with Jesus for me, and that has had a huge impact. You talk about, and live, a relationship with Jesus that is not focused on rule-keeping. Instead, I've seen you model a relationship defined by grace and love and acceptance. Along the way, I've needed people who could understand what was happening to me and guide me into understanding this truth about grace and acceptance. I needed people who could reflect the merciful truth about myself."

And so, we fuel our curiosity about the freedom that defines others in our life. We stay awake and in pursuit mode about what is attractive in others and why it's so attractive to us. As a writer, speaker, and ministry leader, I (Rick) am very attuned to the emotional climate of the other in my life. I mean, I'm hyper-aware of the internal "emotional weather patterns" of the people I encounter. That awareness can make it hard to say and do a hard (but necessary) thing in their lives, because I know they might be hurt by it and reject me as a result.

Several years ago, I was eating breakfast with a pastor I've known for a long time. The time I spend with him is always immersive because the freedom I experience in him soaks into me and exposes my lack of freedom. In the middle of our meal, a man who knew my friend stopped by our table to chat for a moment. About sixty seconds into that innocuous conversation, my friend looked at the visitor and said, "Hey, a woman in the church stopped by my office the other day because she wanted to tell me that she feels uncomfortable around you sometimes. I wanted you to know this, because it's something I think you need to look at." The suddenly flustered man mumbled his goodbyes and shuffled out of the restaurant. My friend turned back to me and picked up our conversation as if nothing had happened. But I stopped him and said, "I can't believe that just happened!" My friend looked at me, smiled, and shrugged his shoulders, as if to say: Dragging things from the darkness into the light is what I do. His freedom, lived out in a restaurant booth where we were surrounded by others, is still a revelation to me and gives me "sonar feedback" about my own captivity. That feedback is a sideways lever, attracting me away from my captivity narratives and toward a more courageous way of giving to others.

The Beliefs We Embrace Are the Beliefs We Become

If we are drawn to the freedom Jesus promises us, our first step on the journey is to acknowledge that we have a story we tell ourselves about ourselves—and that story is fashioned and perpetuated by our beliefs. Jesus made "belief" a primary focus in His ministry because He understands how powerfully our beliefs form our identity. His mission is to restore our identity from broken and captive to whole and free. The heavy lifting that He must do, with our cooperation, is to undermine and replace the destructive narrative our beliefs have formed. Pay attention to how He highlights belief in this volatile interaction with a desperate man:

> One of the men in the crowd spoke up and said, "Teacher,
> I brought my son so you could heal him. He is possessed
> by an evil spirit that won't let him talk. And whenever this
> spirit seizes him, it throws him violently to the ground.
> Then he foams at the mouth and grinds his teeth and
> becomes rigid. So I asked your disciples to cast out the evil
> spirit, but they couldn't do it." Jesus said to them, "You
> faithless people! How long must I be with you? How long
> must I put up with you? Bring the boy to me." So they
> brought the boy. But when the evil spirit saw Jesus, it threw
> the child into a violent convulsion, and he fell to the ground,
> writhing and foaming at the mouth. "How long has this
> been happening?" Jesus asked the boy's father. He replied,
> "Since he was a little boy. The spirit often throws him into
> the fire or into water, trying to kill him. Have mercy on us
> and help us, if you can." "What do you mean, 'If I can'?"
> Jesus asked. "Anything is possible if a person believes." The
> father instantly cried out, "I do believe, but help me over-
> come my unbelief!" (Mark 9:17–24)

In the middle of a charged encounter, with the reality-show crowd watching, Jesus makes this boy's helpless predicament secondary to a much bigger issue—the lack of belief that is hampering the authority and freedom of both His disciples and this needy man. Not only do we become what we believe, but the lives of others are deeply impacted by what we believe about ourselves and what we believe about Jesus.

In the chapters that follow, we'll dig more deeply into a wide array of oblique, sideways strategies that have the power to topple and replace destructive narratives. We'll explore these sideways strategies not as a to-do list, but as a menu of opportunities. You'll love some things on the menu, but not everything will fit your particular life patterns and inclinations. The mission here is simple: When you read and experience something on the menu that resonates for you, be accountable to "take and eat" from that. It's when we take something from outside ourselves (an idea or strategy you read in the following pages) and ingest it (actually experiment with that idea or strategy in your life) that we experience transformation in our life and in the lives of those we love.

In our communion rituals in the church, the celebrant invites the community to ingest the body and blood of Jesus by saying, simply: "Take and eat." Let's walk through the menu that follows, decide on the "food" that resonates, then take and eat.

CHAPTER 6

ENGAGING THE BODY

The Powerful Connections between Physical Habits and Emotional Health and How Jesus Models a Body-Conscious Lifestyle

I n His three-year "public" ministry, Jesus walked an estimated 3,125 miles, and during His lifetime, He likely walked more than 21,000 miles—close to the circumference of the earth.[1] From an early age, He was apprenticed to His father's business as a *tekton* (the Greek word for "craftsman" or "builder"). In most Bible versions, *tekton* is translated as "carpenter," but its actual meaning is closer to "stone mason," because almost all homes at that time in history were constructed out of stone. Nazareth, Jesus's boyhood home, was just three miles from the ancient town of Sepphoris, where King Herod was in the middle of a massive beautification project. *Tektons* were in high demand, working out of the large rock quarry midway between Nazareth and Sepphoris.[2] That quarry likely served as the "office" for Joseph's *tekton* business, where Jesus spent much of His life helping His father lift, cut, and shape heavy stones. This helps explain the many times Jesus used stones and stonemasonry as metaphors in His teaching (Matthew 3:9; 7:9; 21:42–44; 24:2; and Luke 3:8 and 19:40, for example).

The point is that Jesus, in His everyday life, was a physically vigorous man. His muscles ached, His hands were rough, His feet were calloused, and sweat covered His body. He was not the pasty, bunny-soft version of a man we see so often characterized in ancient and contemporary art. The Pharisees and religious leaders would have experienced Him as physically formidable, making His frequent "cage matches" with them even more tense. Though it's true that life in ancient Israel was far more physically demanding in general than our contemporary Western lifestyle (calorie-burning was not an issue), the family business Jesus was born into guaranteed it. That's not a throwaway truth—the Trinity chose this life for the Messiah. A sedentary life was not consistent with "wholly" living.

Engaging our bodies in demanding physical activities represents one "refracted expression" of our love for God and others: "You must love the Lord your God with all your heart, all your soul, all your mind, and all your strength" (Mark 12:30). The "must" in this mission reflects the love in the heart of God. When we give ourselves to Jesus with all our passion and intellect and physicality, we will strengthen our mental health and build up our brain reserve, helping us to overcome the cancerous intent of the destructive narratives planted in our soul.

The Link between Physical Health and Emotional Health

In a study published in the journal *Social Science & Medicine*, researchers found a looping relationship between physical activity and mental health: the more we engage our body, the better equipped we are to face and overcome psychological challenges, and the more we maintain brain health, the more likely we are to be physically active.[3] "Better physical and mental health status...leads to more physical activity," say the study's authors, "which in return has a positive association with better mental health and physical health."

The clear connection between body engagement and a suicide-resistant brain reserve is highlighted in a landmark "gamification" study among residents of Stranraer, Scotland. Researchers challenged community teams to compete for prizes by adopting a much more physically engaged lifestyle. Participants in the "Beat the Street" campaign each registered an "RFID" card online and accumulated points for their team by touching their card to radio scanners called Beat Boxes that were positioned at half-mile intervals around the city. If you touch two Beat Boxes within an hour, you earn ten points for your team. The top-scoring teams could win vouchers for sports equipment, bicycles, and other "active lifestyle" prizes. After the six-week competition, the study's organizers launched a seven-month follow-up campaign to encourage and support the residents of Stranraer to raise the level of their everyday physical activity. The results? A clear, systemic rise in mental wellbeing as a direct result of the city's determination to engage their bodies more regularly. And for those who opted out of the challenge and reported a sedentary lifestyle, their mental wellbeing was "significantly lower."[4]

Yes, it's an over-simplification, but…concrete, demanding physical activity can overshadow and neutralize our emotional wrestling matches. Put another way, the physical pain and challenge brought on by active body engagement can rivet our psychological attention away from our emotional pain, even temporarily, and add to the resolve we need to persevere through our stuck-in-a-pothole seasons of life. When we vigorously engage our bodies, we can break the looping, destructive narrative cycle of our schemas—jumping us out of our emotional rut.

We already know that we have an obesity problem in Western culture. Our screen-obsessed lifestyle has had an obvious and predictable outcome—we are engaging our bodies less and less. The activity guidelines set out for children and young adults by the U.S. Department of Health and Human Services recommends sixty minutes or more of physical activity every day. Most young people get nowhere near that level. And that has coincided with a steep rise in mental health concerns. In a study funded by health insurance giant Blue Cross Blue Shield, researchers found "major depression is on the rise among Americans from all age groups, but is rising fastest among teens and young adults...."[5] This rise in adolescent depression is correlated with a similar rise in screen time and a corresponding fall in activities that support mental health, such as exercise.

Researchers at the University of British Columbia discovered a clear link between screen time and mental health among adolescents: Those who substituted extracurricular activities for sedentary screen habits scored highest on mental health assessments. And, taken alone, two or more hours of screen time after school perpetuated a decline in brain health.[6] Even more troubling, a study published in *Clinical Psychological Science* "found that teens who spent five or more hours a day online were 71 percent more likely than those who spent less than an hour a day to have at least one suicide risk factor (depression, thinking about suicide, making a suicide plan or attempting suicide)." And "suicide risk factors rose significantly after two or more hours a day of time online."[7]

Meanwhile, in a study done by Harvard's School of Public Health, researchers found that "running for fifteen minutes a day or walking for an hour reduces the risk of major depression by 26 percent [and] maintaining an exercise schedule can prevent you from relapsing." The link between body-engaging activities and brain health is strong, broad, and inescapable. So, when we consider the bugs in our hardware and software, it's important to remember that Jesus expects co-participation in our healing—unless we're incapacitated or no longer able to exercise our will. Anything less is disrespectful and diminishing. He lived a vigorous physical life and invited those who follow Him to do the same. That's good news, because there is a way out of the Valley of the Shadow of Death if we will grab the hand of our Guide and put one foot in front of the other.

Make Healthy Body Engagement Your New Norm

Because standard treatment with many antidepressants is now proving to be limited and temporary, researchers are scouting for "natural" alternatives. The link between body engagement and brain health has funneled them back to the habits that fuel a body-fit lifestyle. In a study published in the journal *Reviews in the Neurosciences*, investigators found overwhelming evidence that "exercise improves our mood and is a catalyst for comprehensive benefits affecting our physical health."[8]

Brain plasticity, or the brain's capacity for reprogramming our hardware, is related to "neurogenesis" in the hippocampus region. And a host of scientific studies show that a base level of exercise promotes neurogenesis in adult brains. Simply, we can "rewire" our brain's biology by adopting more body-engaging habits than we do now—that's why the latest research is urging "a new treatment method for depression therapy [that] can be developed by regulating exercise activity." That means "treatment" with exercise can help mild to moderate depression as effectively as antidepressant medication can, without the potential side effects. And exercise represents only the most obvious form of healthy body engagement.

So, how does this translate into our daily life?

• **Walk more, sit less.** Stand, stretch, and move at least once every hour. If you can walk there in ten minutes or less, do that instead of driving or riding public transportation. Get a dog as a pet and you'll be forced to walk way more than you do now. The fitness-monitor craze has set an arbitrary goal of ten thousand steps a day as the standard, but a better interim goal (since most Americans walk far less than ten thousand steps every day) is to boost your steps by a thousand every month until you reach or surpass ten thousand. If you work in an office, take a "lap" around your floor every hour or so. On your lunch break, take a short walk around your building, complex, campus, or block. Take the stairs instead of the elevator—at least once a day. Or take up an activity that requires walking: golf (without a cart), or even mini-golf, frisbee golf, geocaching, hiking, sightseeing, zoo-walking, mall-walking, bird-watching, wildlife photography, hunting, or beachcombing.

• **Eat brain-booster foods.** As we mentioned in Chapter Four, specific foods and dietary supplements help boost brain health. But new research suggests that certain foods help lower anxiety and depression. For example, low levels of magnesium are linked to low levels of serotonin, a natural body chemical that helps stabilize our mood. Magnesium also works at the cellular level to help block stress hormones from gaining access to the brain. Magnesium-rich foods include eggs, spinach, chard, pumpkin seeds, dry roasted almonds, cashews, black beans, dark chocolate, avocados, and peanut butter. In addition, foods rich in antioxidants or Vitamin B can help boost our brain reserve. Oxidative stress contributes to inflammation in our brain, inhibiting neurotransmitter production, and destabilizing our mood. So try eating more blueberries, blackberries, strawberries, brussels sprouts, broccoli, and spinach. Higher levels of Vitamin B are proven to boost the mood of those struggling with depression or anxiety; avocados, almonds, and eggs are all great sources.

Here's the kicker: new research shows "gut bacteria" play a significant role in our mental health. Studies show a connection between consumption of probiotic yogurt and lower levels of stress that leads to anxiety and depression. The same is true for other fermented foods, including kombucha, pickles, and sauerkraut.

• **Change your sleep habits.** People who are wrestling with mental health problems and are caught up in the spiral of destructive narratives often have problems sleeping. Conventional wisdom has treated sleep disruptions as symptoms of psychological distress, but new research suggests the opposite is likely truer: troubled sleep habits actually cause people to descend into the darkness. In a Harvard

Medical School report on "Sleep and Mental Health," investigators report that "sleep disruption—which affects levels of neurotransmitters and stress hormones, among other things—wreaks havoc in the brain, impairing thinking and emotional regulation."[9] And the same Harvard researchers found that people with a history of insomnia are four times as likely to develop depression. Sleep problems are a precursor to major depression, not the result of it. Here's how you can develop sleep-healthy habits:

- *Follow your sleep rhythms, not the clock.* Babies who have trouble sleeping through the night can break that cycle if their parent(s) will notice and respond to their sleep rhythms. When a baby is ready for sleep, he/she will exhibit a short interlude (five or ten minutes) of calm—like the eye of a hurricane. The face goes blank, and the stare is fixed and far-off. Put that baby to bed during that marker moment, and he/she has a much better chance of sleeping through the night. It works. I (Rick) tried it with our second sleep-challenged daughter, and it changed everything. And we don't "grow out of" this sleep-friendly rhythm. If you become more aware of your own "calm interlude," note when it usually happens, then get to bed at around that time every night and you'll sleep better.
- *Cut out the blue wavelengths in light.* Blue light suppresses your body's ability to prepare for sleep by blocking melatonin, a hormone that makes you sleepy. Use blue light-blocking glasses, activate night-mode on your devices, cut back on screen time, or swap out LED bulbs with incandescent bulbs (or amber-colored LED bulbs) to cut out the blue range of light that is responsible for keeping us awake.

○ *Follow a comforting routine.* Again, just as babies love sleep-time rituals, so do young people and adults. The short version of this is to do whatever is soothing to you. Read something light, listen to nature sounds or white noise, look back on the day and write a short list of things you're grateful for, give your pet some attention, snuggle, take a hot shower or bath, or watch the monologue from your favorite late-night show (no more than that, because the "cold" light of a TV can delay sleep).

○ *Alter harmful habits.* If you have a clock in your room, consider turning it away before you close your eyes; clock-watching can increase your stress. And put your phone and computer away for the night an hour before bedtime—that notorious blue light is an enemy of sleep. Make sure your bedroom light is dim or can be dimmed easily. Instead of chewing on anxious, stressful, or "got to remember that" thoughts, keep a notepad next to your bed to write them down, so you can "release" them. And make sure your bedroom is cool, not warm—somewhere between sixty and sixty-seven degrees is best, according to sleep researchers.

• **Practice non-traditional exercise.** If you're burned out on traditional fitness regimens (another way of saying "running"), try something creative and new. Play *Just Dance* with friends or your spouse on the Wii video gaming system, sign up for historic walking tours or walkable home-shows, get involved in a crafting hobby that requires you to use your hands (researchers have discovered that painting, woodworking, a cooking class, or knitting reinforce our "hand-brain connection," giving our brains the fitness workout it craves), play "cross movement" sports that involve both your arms and legs (such as running, rock-climbing, paddle-boating, swimming, skiing, step classes, mountain biking, or weight-lifting), or circumvent the high cost of a round of golf and hit a bucket of balls at a lower-cost golfing range. Also, consider body-movement "Contrology" exercises, such as Pilates (in a class or following one of the hundreds of online instructors)—it's been shown to reduce anxiety nearly as well as cognitive behavioral therapy.[10]

The "Secret Weapon" of Body Engagement

When economist Julius Ohrnberger and his team at the University of Manchester's Centre for Health Economics decided to study the impact of physical activity on mental wellbeing, they added a "mediator" into the mix—social contact. And they discovered that social interaction acts like a kind of multiplier, boosting the brain-reserve power of exercise in a small but significant way. Anecdotally, more and more fitness centers are spotlighting "team" approaches to fitness that build community while they build muscle mass and endurance. The social interactions produced by facing and overcoming physical challenges can lead to deep and lasting relationships, and that relational capital magnifies the mental health benefits of body engagement. According to a survey by the American College of Sports Medicine, "Group Training" is third on its list of international fitness trends.[11] Health clubs are adding group cycling and treadmill classes that feature group dynamics, along with the step and aerobic classes most already offer. This trend is also reflected in the rise of socially connected exercise machines such as Peloton and Hydrow. This social-contact "multiplier" boosts engagement, motivation, and reward.

So, when you're walking, running, lifting, climbing, cycling, crafting, swimming, or dancing, follow this simple multiplier strategy: Invite a friend. God is three persons in one (we call this the Trinity) for a reason. Community is at the core of God's identity, and community helps us maximize the impact of body engagement.

WHAT YOU CAN DO IF ...

You're the One Who's Struggling	You Care for Someone Who's Struggling
• Walk 10 minutes more per day than you do now.	• Every day, offer to walk or do something that involves movement with your friend or loved one.
• Add more eggs, spinach, chard, pumpkin seeds, dry roasted almonds, cashews, black beans, dark chocolate, avocados, and peanut butter to your diet. And try eating more blueberries, blackberries, strawberries, brussels sprouts, and broccoli.	• When you serve food or order food or give gifts of food, use this as your "menu of options": eggs, spinach, chard, pumpkin seeds, dry roasted almonds, cashews, black beans, dark chocolate, avocados, peanut butter, blueberries, blackberries, strawberries, brussels sprouts, and broccoli.
• Get on a regular sleep rhythm, turn off your screens thirty minutes before bedtime, use incandescent or amber-colored light bulbs, and use white noise to lull you to sleep.	• Give a white-noise machine or blue-light-blocking glasses or an alarm clock that dims the lighted numbers as a gift to your friend or family member.
• Play *Just Dance* on the Wii video gaming system, go on a walking tour, get involved in a crafting hobby, play a "cross movement" sport that involve both your arms and legs, try Pilates, or hit a bucket of balls at a golfing range.	• Join a fitness club with your friend or family member and sign up for a "regular" class (or classes) together. Offer to go together to the club to maintain consistency.

CHAPTER 7

IMMERSING IN THE NATURAL WORLD

**Why the Apostle Paul Emphasizes the Importance
of Our Connection to the Natural World and How to
"Practice the Presence" of Nature**

My (Rick's) wife has an immune deficiency that long ago kick-started a lung disease called sarcoidosis. Because of an experimental treatment and a brilliant immunologist, its advance was stopped fifteen years ago. Her doctor's strategy and immunoglobulin treatment, along with her own host of "wholly living" practices, have so far kept the monster at bay. Bev is a learner and a doer, so she experiments with a wide variety of fitness, diet, and supplement strategies to help keep sarcoidosis in its cage. That's why she's recently taken up running again. Her joints can't handle the hard pavement of our neighborhood streets, so she runs on a beautiful, forested city trail that's just minutes from our house. It's one of the country's longest (seventy-one miles) and most-used nature trails (half a million people use it every year). Lately, I've altered my own fitness routine to join her on the trail, just to be a support. In the past, when I've run on the two-mile asphalt loop that circles our neighborhood, I've struggled to finish without stopping. Usually, I stop once or twice to walk. But I've discovered that on a four-mile loop along a forested stream, I can run without stopping the whole way. How is this possible? Is it fairy dust drifting down on me from the trees?

That sounds ridiculous, but it's actually not far from the truth.

For decades in Japan, millions have practiced "forest bathing"—regular "immersion" in forested environments—as a wellness strategy. To understand why this practice has such a profound effect on participants' brain health, researchers in Japan spent four million dollars studying the impact of forested trails on "human natural killer" (NK) cells, the SWAT team members of our immune system. They discovered that *Shinrin-yoku* (prolonged exposure to trees) reduces stress and depression, boosts the strength of NK cells, and drops blood pressure. It turns out that trees do emit fairy dust, better known as essential oils, or phytoncides. Trees fill the air with these oils to protect themselves from germs and insects; when we inhale phytoncides, they improve our immune system's function and, by extension, our mental health.

Dr. Viren Swami, a professor of social psychology at Anglia Ruskin University in the United Kingdom, says: "English populations with the most green space in their surroundings also have the lowest levels of mortality. The simple fact is that people tend to be healthier and live longer when they have easy access to nature. Accessible green space is also good for our psychological well-being. For example, large-scale surveys in the Netherlands[1] and UK[2] have shown that individuals living in urban areas with more green space have lower rates of mental health distress and are more satisfied with life than those living in areas with less green space. Other studies show that exposure to natural environments reduces negative emotions[3]—including anger, anxiety, and sadness."[4] And when the authors of a study published in the journal *Environment and Behavior* set out to discover the impact of our "attachment" to nature, they found a clear connection between the natural world's "ability to fulfill the basic psychological needs of autonomy, competence, and relatedness" and a depression-resistant lifestyle.[5]

For creaky, sporadic runners like my wife and me, forest bathing has had the same impact my PF Flyers had when I was a kid—we can "run faster and jump higher." But it's also adding to our depression-fighting brain reserve. It's no accident that the natural world, created and infiltrated by God, is perpetually working to heal us and restore us and defend us—whether or not we know it. In Chapter Three ("Debugging Our Operating System"), we slowed down to pay attention to a remarkable truth about nature the Apostle Paul revealed near the start of his letter to the early Christians living in Rome. All of creation, he says, is imbued with the personality and power of God. So, when we "bathe" in nature, we're literally immersing ourselves in the (not just metaphoric) presence of God (Romans 1:20). The poem that launches John's gospel reminds us, "The Word [gives] life to everything that was created, and his life [brings] light to everyone" (John 1:4). When we spend time in the natural world, we are breathing in life and pushing away death.

Practicing the Presence of Nature

In a study of almost five hundred healthy volunteers, researchers recorded psychological "temperature checks" when participants were in a forested environment and then when they were in a "control" environment. When the volunteers "practiced the presence of nature," scientists discovered steep reductions in feelings of hostility and depression and steep hikes in feelings of "liveliness." Their conclusion: "This study revealed that forest environments are advantageous with respect to acute emotions, especially among those experiencing chronic stress."[6] As with all of the ideas you'll read in Part Two of this book, "nature immersion" is just one of many options on the brain-reserve menu. The possibilities range from simple to more complex, so pursue what sounds intriguing, take a chance on something you've never tried before, and leave the rest for another season in your life.

1. **Go barefoot more often.** Sure, barefoot living (called "earthing" by some adherents) is a non-starter in many of our everyday environments, but the next time you're near a grassy area, a park, a forest, a lake, or the ocean, take off your shoes and walk for a bit. Barefoot walking helps regulate the nervous system, strengthens your immune system, and reduces feelings of stress and anxiety. The tactile experience of stimulating your feet in natural environments wakes up the brain's vestibular system (regulating balance) and stimulates new neural connections that encourage improved brain health. Plus, researchers have discovered that barefoot-to-earth contact actually stimulates healthy electrical activity in the brain, essentially completing the electrical circuit between our body and the earth's electrical field (no kidding!).[7] This increased activity adds to our brain reserve, helping us move into and out of the potholes we encounter in life.

2. **Spend at least twenty minutes every day outside.** In a study published in the *Journal of Environmental Psychology*, researchers found that a minimal daily investment in outdoor exposure (just twenty minutes) significantly boosted "vitality"—the life-energizing fuel at our psychological core. Richard Ryan, professor of psychology at the University of Rochester and an author of the study, says, "Research has shown that people with a greater sense of vitality don't just have more energy for things they want to do, they are also more resilient...."[8] The COVID-19 pandemic leveraged a shift toward a work-at-home norm in our culture, and that opens up opportunities for living and working outside that didn't seem practical before. Move your mobile office outdoors for an hour every morning, or tote your laptop to a park for a stretch, or drive to a forested area and set up on a picnic table for the afternoon. If you're tied to an office environment, walk to get lunch instead of driving, or start a lunchtime walking club, or take a short break from your grind and take your bicycle out on a city trail for thirty minutes. If you're a city-dweller, find a nearby park or open space and do some stretching or birdwatching, or simply

wander as you breathe deeply. Try the "twenty minutes outdoors" strategy every day for a week—your soul will then crave your new "outdoor diet" and give you a nudge when you need it.

Before the COVID-19 lockdown protocols, I (Daniel) routinely took a short walk at lunch during my workday. But then, after my office moved to my home, I found other things to do during that lunch window—like responding to emails. It took a few weeks before the impact of these lost walks started to take a toll on my body. I developed backaches and ended each week feeling more stressed. But then, on a weekend walk with my wife and young daughter on a trail near our home, I felt refueled. And I remembered how important walking has been to my own brain health. Simple practices can have a profound effect on our wellbeing when they become routine.

3. Join an outdoor social/fitness group. Go to Meetup.com and search for "Outdoor Fitness Groups" in your area. The site will automatically suggest groups near your ZIP code. This idea is a two-fer: you get the psychological benefits of nature-immersion in the context of brain-boosting social connections. In the era of social distancing, many more health clubs and fitness centers are offering outdoor classes, and some have long offered outdoor "boot camps" that are gender-specific. If you're on Facebook, search for "Outdoor Fitness/Adventure Groups" and pore over your options. Join a weekend recreational cycling group that frequents bike paths that will take you through natural surroundings. Or, if you're looking for something even more adventurous, find a trail-running group, open-water swimming group, horseback-riding group, or even an obstacle-course racing group in your area.

4. Garden. When comedian and actor Jim Gaffigan was trying to find a way to exercise some agency over the uncontrollable impact of the COVID-19 pandemic restrictions, the lifelong city-dweller turned to a surprising (and ancient) practice—gardening. In a piece produced for *CBS Sunday Morning*, Gaffigan says:

I blame the house we rented...I noticed the rental house had some raised garden beds. I thought, okay, we'll plant some seeds. That's something the kids can do while I nap. Well, the kids lost interest immediately, but I continued to water and tend and, well, garden. Through gardening I found something I couldn't get from binge-watching, a Zoom meeting, or even a cheeseburger. I acquired control. Well, some control. Obviously I can't control a global pandemic. But I can plant a seed, make sure it gets water, and grow something where there used to just be dirt. It's not just the accomplishment of growing something that wasn't there. It's the autonomy. It's something I did during the pandemic by myself.

In a study published in the *British Medical Journal*, Australian researcher Dr. Paul Biegler cites "greater personal autonomy" as a significant and effective way to combat the downward pressure of anxiety and depression.[9] That means Gaffigan's sense that greater autonomy (planting things and watching them grow) gave him a stronger foundation to face the stressors brought on by the pandemic is spot-on. Add to this the added benefit of outdoor immersion and the inherent tactile connections with the earth, and gardening offers strong therapeutic help for those struggling to counter their destructive narratives.

5. **Bring the outdoors indoors.** Sit near a window when you're working or reading so you can expose yourself to nature. Or use headphones or earbuds to listen to nature sounds. In a study published by *Scientific Reports*, researchers used a functional MRI scanner to measure brain activity in volunteers as they listened to recorded sounds from either natural or artificial environments. Natural sounds drew listeners' attention outward in a manner similar to the brain activity caused by daydreaming. Artificial sounds did

the opposite, creating an "inner digging" momentum that mapped to the same brain rhythms characteristic of anxiety, post-traumatic stress disorder, and depression.

If possible, bring more plants and indoor shrubs into your home. Buy sale or clearance fresh-cut flowers and make them a permanent fixture in your kitchen or eating area. Consider decorating in earth-and-sky tones that suggest the naturally occurring colors of the outdoors (in "color theory," blues and greens create a calming atmosphere). Colorists also recommend dark stains on wood floors to mimic the effect that soil has on our psychology. Wood furniture that is naturally stained is also a subtle way to bring the outdoors inside. Try decorating with fruits and vegetables or framing shells or flowers or other specimens from nature and mounting them on your walls. It's more time-consuming, expensive, and elaborate, but installing skylights or adding windows will bathe your home in more natural light.

6. Just add water. In a *USA Today* interview, marine biologist Wallace J. Nichols, author of the bestselling book *Blue Mind*, says:

> The term "blue mind" describes the mildly meditative state we fall into when near, in, on, or under water. It's the antidote to what we refer to as "red mind," which is the anxious, over-connected and over-stimulated state that defines the new normal of modern life. Research has proven that spending time near the water is essential to achieving an elevated and sustained happiness.... Being near, in, on, or under water can provide a long list of benefits for our mind and body, including lowering stress and anxiety, increasing an overall sense of well-being and happiness, a lower heart and breathing rate, and safe, better workouts. Aquatic therapists are increasingly looking to the water to help treat and manage PTSD, addiction, anxiety disorders, autism and more.

The premise Nichols sets out to prove in his book is simple: "sitting by the water quietly is really good for you...."

Of course, if you live near an ocean the opportunities for feeding your "blue mind" are easy to envision—walking on the beach, swimming, snorkeling, boogie-boarding, surfing, scuba diving, fishing, and boating. But Nichols emphasizes that "water therapy" is possible wherever you can find a natural source—almost three-quarters of the world's population (70 percent) lives within five kilometers of water (rivers, streams, lakes, and ponds). The goal is simply to get near enough to the water to touch it, then unplug from distractions and get quiet. The touch, smell, and sound of water is therapeutic and has a restorative impact on our psychological health. According to environmental psychologist Dr. Mathew White of the University of Exeter, spending time in and around aquatic environments strengthens a positive mood and reduces negative moods and stress—even more than green spaces do.[10]

Consider the Lilies

Stanford's Dr. Gregory Bratman and his colleagues randomly assigned sixty participants to a fifty-minute walk in either a natural setting (a forested area) or an urban setting (along a four-lane road). Before and after the walk, Bratman collected data on their emotional and cognitive state. Those who were assigned the nature walk experienced less anxiety, rumination (focused, negative attention on yourself), and negative affect compared to the urban walkers. In another study, Bratman zeroed in on the natural world's impact on rumination specifically because of its connection to anxiety and depression. Using functional MRI technology, researchers observed that natural settings decreased rumination and increased activity in the "subgenual prefrontal cortex," the brain region that helps regulate depression and anxiety. Our immersion in natural settings is not the cherry on top of our mental-health sundae—it's a scoop of fudge-ripple ice cream itself!

In Luke 12, Jesus is trying to help His disciples embrace a new way of thinking and living—a life-giving, wholly living lifestyle that reflects the values and norms of the Kingdom of God, not the kingdom of mankind. So He asks them to "consider" nature as a teacher: "Consider the lilies, how they grow: they neither toil nor spin; but I tell you, not even Solomon in all his glory clothed himself like one of these. But if God so clothes the grass in the field, which is alive today and tomorrow is thrown into the furnace, how much more will He clothe you? (Luke 12:27–28 NASB). The Greek word translated "consider" here means "to examine closely" or "to learn thoroughly." It is an unusual word for Jesus to use—He's trying to emphasize the deep impact nature can have on the way we interpret our story and live out our identity. He wants us to invite the healing, restoring, redeeming power of the natural world into our everyday life.

WHAT YOU CAN DO IF . . .

You're the One Who's Struggling	You Care for Someone Who's Struggling
• Whenever possible, whenever you're outside, go barefoot for a few minutes.	• Whenever possible, when you're with your friend or loved one outside, playfully ask: "Can we just take our shoes off and walk for a bit?"
• Make a list of outside environments that are easily accessible for you (patio, park, porch, rooftop) and replace one "inside time" every day with one "outside time."	• Ask your coworker or friend or family member to "get a breath of fresh air" with you every day. Walk to get coffee or to walk a pet or to run a "walkable" errand together.

• Go to Meetup.com and find an outdoor-based group to join.	• With your friend or loved one, find an outdoor-based group on Meetup.com or Facebook that you can join together.
• Start a small outdoor garden in a large pot or small plot of ground. Start by planting flower or vegetable seeds.	• Give your friend or loved one a "garden-starter" kit—you can find many options by simply searching for "garden-starter kit" on Amazon.com.
• Whenever you're sitting indoors, move to the seat that's closest to an outside window.	• Give your friend or loved one a nature-themed decoration that fits with the person's home or office décor.
• For a family vacation or outing, prioritize being near water.	• Suggest water-related activities to your friend or loved one, including a walk or hike near a lake or stream, swimming, or boating. Sit together next to a fountain or waterfall for conversation and coffee.

CHAPTER 8

PAYING ATTENTION TO THE PRESENT

**How Our Obsessions about the Future and the Past
Drive Us into the Darkness and How a Mindful Fixation
on the Present Moment Offers Us Light**

At the end of the farewell episode for her popular and top-rated TV talk show, Oprah Winfrey condensed all that she'd learned about people over the course of her twenty-five-year run into a startling summation. With tears welling in her eyes, she stared into the camera and said: "I've talked to nearly thirty thousand people on this show, and all thirty thousand had one thing in common: they all wanted validation. If I could reach through this television and sit on your sofa or sit on a stool in your kitchen right now, I would tell you that every single person you will ever meet shares that common desire. They want to know: 'Do you see me? Do you hear me? Does what I say mean anything to you?'"

What all people everywhere are longing for is for someone to be present to their beauty—their made-in-the-image-of-God "real self." But we rarely give others the gift of our full attention, and (even more convicting) we are rarely present to ourselves. We are a validation-starved people.

Gina Biegel, a psychotherapist and founder of Stressed Teens (stressedteens.com), studies young people who've sought counseling to help them with their stress. She says most are oblivious to the impact of their tech-saturated environment and the almost-constant noise it produces in their lives. "Teens are really never in silence," she told CNN. "They never have this moment just to be with their thoughts, be with who they are and actually what that feels like, to learn how to be comfortable by yourself." To help release the stress building up in their souls, Biegel helps overwhelmed and suicidal teenagers learn "mindfulness" techniques. And she's seen a profound reduction in anxiety, depression, obsessive symptoms, and interpersonal problems.

"Mindfulness" can sound like a made-up word invented by the New Age movement. While it's true that the practice gained popularity as an offshoot of Buddhist meditation, at its core it's a "wholly living" imperative rooted in the teaching and lifestyle-modeling of Jesus. Ellen Langer, a Harvard psychologist and author of *Mindfulness*, describes the practice as a slow-down-and-pay-attention lifestyle that not only reduces the "tinder" that fuels our psychological forest fires, but also helps us maintain our focus on the present moment, rather than obsessing over the past or future. "When you're being mindful," says Langer, "you're simply noticing new things. Mindfulness is what you're doing when you're at leisure. [For example] if you are on a vacation, you're looking for new things. It's enjoyable rather than taxing. It's mostly energy-begetting, not energy-consuming."[1] The American Psychological Association defines mindfulness as "a moment-to-moment awareness of one's experience without judgment. In this sense, mindfulness is a state and not a trait." And the editors of *Psychology Today* describe it as "a state of active, open attention on the present."

Small children are naturally mindful—they live in the present moment as if the past and future don't exist. They are fully invested in the now and are militantly unconcerned about the not-now. They don't account for the external realities of life because they're fixated on the treasure box of this moment in time. When my (Rick's) daughter Emma was ten, she came home from school positively evangelistic about her friend's upcoming trip to Hawaii. She excitedly described the nirvana-like experiences her friend was about to enjoy in paradise, then asked, as if she were requesting a glass of water, "When will we be going to Hawaii?" When I responded, "Right now, that's asking for way too much," her eyes clouded over with confusion. If an experience on a tropical island promised that much fun, what could possibly be "too much" about it? If we give way to condescension in situations like these, we give our kids an "adult smile" and put their unreasonable, unrealistic expectations to shame. They don't understand or acknowledge the dragons we must slay as adults—the mortgage, the grocery bills, and the car repairs—so we discount and disrespect their worldview.

But this natural "bent" in children is, in large part, why Jesus upended and challenged conventional attitudes about them:

> One day some parents brought their little children to Jesus so he could touch and bless them. But when the disciples saw this, they scolded the parents for bothering him. Then Jesus called for the children and said to the disciples, "Let the children come to me. Don't stop them! For the Kingdom of God belongs to those who are like these children. I tell you the truth, anyone who doesn't receive the Kingdom of God like a child will never enter it." (Luke 18:15–17)

The Kingdom of God is the "native culture" of the Trinity; it's a way of describing how things work in the "hometown" of the Father, Son, and Holy Spirit. So, to "enter" the Kingdom of God means to accept and embrace the lifestyle, worldview, and priorities that Jesus modeled. And children, He says, already practice these values naturally.

In the Kingdom of God ...	But in the kingdom of the world ...
• We can be "anxious for nothing" because we are intimately connected to a good God who cares for us.	• We must be anxious about everything, because tragedy and trauma can strike at any moment, and our sole protection is our own agency.
• We learn, as the Apostle Paul did, "to live on almost nothing or with everything" (Philippians 4:11).	• We must plan and scheme and strive for our future happiness, because no one will do that for us.
• We live in the redemptive passion of Jesus, which enables us to "turn the page" on our past and find joy in the present.	• We refuse to release our past, continually returning to the "brackish well-water" of our history, hoping our thirst will finally be quenched.
• We are convinced that "nothing can ever separate us from God's love...neither our fears for today nor our worries about tomorrow..." (Romans 8:38).	• We borrow stress from the future, because anxiety and worry offer themselves as a bastardized form of control over the unknown and the uncontrollable.

Surrendering to the Present

Steve Merritt, a counselor and university professor, tells a profound (and metaphoric) story about the impact of childlike mindfulness—investing ourselves in present-dependence, not worry, anxiety, and control:

A four-foot cable hangs on my office wall, directly above my desk. The wires are all frayed and broken in the middle, except for a single strand. Although this object isn't particularly decorative, my life depends on the story behind it. In 1942, my dad was a captain in the U.S. Air Force. Right before he and his crew were about to depart Iceland for the transatlantic flight to England, my dad asked for an inspection of his C-47. The wire on my wall is that plane's rudder cable. The one small strand reveals how close my dad and his crew came to dying in the northern Atlantic's frigid waters.

That cable reminds me I'm not in control. It calls out for dependency and a willingness to constantly trust God. James 4:13–14 reminds us we don't know what will happen in the next few minutes, let alone tomorrow, next week, or next year. The message is that we aren't in charge. Not knowing how many tomorrows will come leads some people to live each day to the fullest. They remind me of the *Calvin and Hobbes* cartoon where Calvin worries, "It's the first week of summer, and we aren't having enough fun yet!" This perspective can subtly lead us to strive or perform, always wondering if we're living well enough in the moment. Such effort becomes another form of wanting control.

Dependency, meanwhile, involves waving the white flag to control. It's a form of surrender and, this side of heaven, usually doesn't show up without a fight. My natural direction is control, not dependency. So I need the single strand on my wall to state emphatically, "It's not about you. It's about Me. I haven't guaranteed your life. Live each day leaning on Me."[2]

The operative word Merritt uses in his story is "surrender"—living mindfully (or openly and intentionally) relative to the present moment, rather than investing ourselves in the anxious demands of our destructive narratives. It's a conscious, surrendering shift of trust from our own "saving behavior" to the rescuing "good shepherd" who "sacrifices his life for the sheep" (John 10:11). We can be present to the here-and-now because our past has been redeemed (artfully repurposed from something ugly to something beautiful), and our future is in the hands of a God who will take care of it for us.

Sophia* is struggling to resist the gravitational pull of the darkness in her life. She's wearing what amounts to reverse-blinders: She cannot see what is right in front of her—the present moment—because the past and the future are clouding her perspective and fueling her spiral. In the slipstream of the COVID-19 pandemic, she's desperately fighting to keep her head above water, and she writes this prayer in her journal:

> I'm aware of my great need for You, Jesus. I have longed to be held in Your arms and comforted by You. I am in desperate need of Your love and grace and help. I need You, Jesus. Even in the air I breathe, I desperately need You. The pandemic and all that surrounds it has left a hurricane storm swirling around us. I've never been through anything so upending. It's made me think about death and sickness way too much. I watch the impact on my kids and I hurt so much for them—for all they have and will lose. The future is uncertain. Dave's job situation is unknown. Finances unknown. Will I get COVID eventually anyway? Will I ever go back to the health club? To church? Please help me get my emotional stuff worked out. Be the solid rock under my feet. I'm tired of being at sea in the storm.

What Sophia needs, but can't yet articulate, is a childlike attention to the grace and provision and advocacy of Jesus in her present moment. He does not promise the "manna" of His sustenance outside of the needs we have today. Put another way, our best defense against the assaulting terrors of the past and the future is a mindful commitment to live in the now. "So don't worry about tomorrow," Jesus says, "for tomorrow will bring its own worries. Today's trouble is enough for today" (Matthew 6:34).

Living in the Present

In the awkward moments after Jesus asks His friend Peter if he loves Him, three times over, the reconciled disciple is walking the sand on the beach of the Sea of Galilee with his beloved for the last time. Jesus has just told Peter that his future will include a horrible sacrifice—He will die on a cross, crucified for His undaunting and unwavering love. It is what Peter has always vowed he would endure for the sake of the Messiah, and now he knows he'll get his wish. But instead of staying in that present moment, in the grace-full now of Jesus's sweet presence, "Peter turned around and saw behind them the disciple Jesus loved— the one who had leaned over to Jesus during supper and asked, 'Lord, who will betray you?' Peter asked Jesus, 'What about him, Lord?' Jesus replied, 'If I want him to remain alive until I return, what is that to you? As for you, follow me'" (John 21:20-22). When Jesus lightly rebukes Peter with "what is that to you?," He is dragging him back from the future into the present. I am inviting you to fully invest yourself in this moment, this conversation, this last intimacy between us...Be here, Peter.

In our own present moment, Jesus is inviting us to rivet our attention on the grace He has laid at our feet. If we will pick up that grace, we will begin to blunt the tyranny of the past and the future, and we will protect our beleaguered soul from shouldering a weight it can't sustain.

1. **Follow a past/present/future soul diet.** Think about your relationship with the past, present, and future as if you're planning a balanced, healthy diet for your soul every day. The present is your main course—make it your primary soul food. The past, then, is a small side dish, and the future is an even smaller dessert to top off your "meal." Consider, also, the "nutritional value" of each component in this meal:

- Think of your main course, the present, as if it's your favorite meal—a savory plate of chicken piccata, for example. When you "eat" the present, savor every taste. Slow down to notice beauty in the people and environment of your everyday life. Stop to thank Jesus for the "little mercies" of your day. Beauty is always in the details, so pay attention to things you normally take for granted and whisper appreciation for them (the pet curled up on your lap, a gentle breeze in the evening, a friend who reaches out to connect, a favorite song you haven't heard in a while—anything). Remember what you love about your life, the evidence of grace all around you, and the way you've been rescued and redeemed. When you sense you are sliding into old patterns or feel dragged back into the "cellar" of your destructive narrative, stop and notice your present surroundings—the lighting, the colors in the room, the sounds, the smells. Rivet your attention in your present environment because it's in your present environment that you can "taste and see" the grace Jesus is offering you.
- Think about your side dish, the past, as a complementary "flavor" to your main course. Spend little time "eating" from your past and do it only to appreciate more fully the present, or to bring your past to Jesus for

healing. Make your side-dish tastes of the past easy to eat—no tough-textured foods that you have to chew and chew to swallow (unless some of your past has remained "unprocessed" in your soul, and chewing on it will help you finally leave it behind). Do not make the past your main course in life—either by elevating and romanticizing it, or by demonizing it. For example, if you look back on your high school or college days as your "high point" in life, then you've elevated your side dish to the main course. Conversely, if you've defined your identity by the trauma of your past, you've given it an out-sized power to shape you.

• Think about your dessert, the future, as the cap to your soul meal—something you can relish, but only in small portions. If you anticipate darkness on your horizon, stare at it only long enough to reasonably and faithfully prepare for it—to steel yourself in the present for the challenges you see coming in the future. Or, if you see a promised joy on your horizon, don't stop to drill a well in that mythical oasis. When we attempt to extract life in the present from a future that is yet to be, we are racking up debts that reality will have a hard time paying. If we set up camp in the land of future possibilities, we are anchoring our life on sand, and "when the rains and floods come and the winds beat against that house, it will collapse with a mighty crash" (Matthew 7:27).

The nature of God is "other" than us, yet still reflected in us: "Let us make human beings in our image, to be like us" (Genesis 1:26). Because God "lives outside of time," the past, present, and future are all present to Him. That means the present is God's only reality, and when we make the present our main course in life, we reflect His nature most profoundly.

2. Whenever possible, live in sensory slow-down mode. Pastor, author, and leadership consultant Tom Melton calls himself an "apprecianado"— a mash-up of "appreciation" and "aficionado." An apprecianado, he says, is a savor-er, someone who pays quality and quantity attention to the sensory nuances around him. And how do we see Jesus modeling this approach to life? Well, He never misses a moment of beauty—from the widow nobody noticed dropping her "mite" into the collection pot, to the "woman with an issue of blood" who touched Him in a desperate attempt to find healing, to the "ravens [that] don't plant or harvest or store food in barns" and the "lilies [that] don't work or make their clothing" (Luke 12:24–27). Jesus pays close attention to the wonderful, the beautiful, and the extraordinary all around Him—then finds active ways to embrace and express what He experiences. People who embrace the perspective of an apprecianado treat beauty with the humility of a child, slowing down to take in the joy of it, recognizing when something big and great (but often quite small) is happening.

What does it mean to slow down and live as an apprecianado in sensory slow-down mode? G. K. Chesterton said: "Poets do not go mad, but chess players do." He's encouraging the exercise of our "appreciation muscles" as a brain-health strategy—the slow, thoughtful contemplation of the beauty around us.

- Sight: Pause often in the midst of your day to focus your gaze on one small detail in your life—let your eyes rest on it for a full thirty seconds. What memories does that small thing tap into for you? How do the colors of it impact you? Why are you grateful for the thing itself, or what it represents? How does it remind you of Jesus? Relax as you rest your gaze: "Cease striving and know that I am God" (Psalm 46:10).

- Sound: Close your eyes every now and then and spend thirty seconds simply listening to the sounds around you. Try to focus on one sound in particular—what emotions does that sound produce in you? How does it make you feel? What memories of childhood does it conjure for you? What blessings in your life does it remind you of? Listen to your favorite music and see if you can isolate just one instrument in the song and enjoy it separate from the others.

- Smell: Close your eyes and take a big, deep breath in through your nose—do this four times, slowly. What do you smell that you like, and why? Dislike? What impact does that smell have on your stress right now? What memories from important times in your childhood does that smell connect to (the holidays or birthdays, for example)? Metaphorically, how does that smell remind you of Jesus? For example, the light and tender smell of flowers can remind us of the shockingly tender way Jesus elevated and encouraged the broken and needy people around Him. Focus on the air going in and out of your nose.

- Touch: With your eyes closed, rest your hand on something nearby. Explore that surface with your fingers for fifteen seconds. What emotions do you feel as you explore? What challenges or joys in your life does that touch remind you of? What else does the feel of that surface remind you of? If you had to make up a word that describes the sensation of that touch, what would it be?

- Taste: At your next meal, eat twice as slowly as you normally do. Tell the cook (even if it's you) what nuances of taste you're picking up as you savor. Express your gratefulness to the cook for the subtle ways the food you're eating has been prepared—the texture, complexity, and even temperature of your meal. Ask Jesus to remind you of the last time you tasted those tastes and who you were with at the time. In Romans 1, Paul reminds us that all of creation is infused with the characteristics of God—so taste something, then silently ask Jesus to show you which of His characteristics that taste is most like. If it's savory, for example, we might be reminded of the "thick and deep and rich" way people like Zacchaeus experienced Jesus.

3. **Practice "Lectio Divina."** The ancient monastic tradition of Lectio Divina (Latin for "Divine Reading") is a "practice of scriptural reading, meditation, and prayer intended to promote communion with God…."[3] It's a perfect way to slow down and be more present to the presence of God as you read Scripture, focusing your attention on the here and now of His voice, rather than merely increasing your knowledge. Here's how it works:

- Choose a text you'd like to focus on. Any text is okay, as long as the goal isn't to "cover" a large chunk of Scripture.
- Get comfortable and silence your "inner conversation." Some Christians focus for a few moments on their breathing, while others have a beloved "prayer word" or "prayer phrase" they gently recite, just as an aid in quieting their soul. Use whatever "silencing" method is best for you.
- Turn to the text and read it slowly and gently. Savor each portion of the reading, constantly listening for the "still, small voice" of the Holy Spirit. In Lectio Divina, Jesus is teaching us to listen to Him—to seek Him in silence.

Read the passage aloud, and just listen. Then read the passage in conversation with Jesus, highlighting anything He wants you to notice. Then read only the highlighted portions—ask Jesus what He wants to show you.

- Repeat the highlighted phrases to yourself. Memorize them and slowly repeat them to yourself—let them interact with your concerns, memories, and ideas. Do not be afraid of distractions. When a memory or thought surfaces, embrace it and give it over to Jesus.

- Tell Jesus how the passage is impacting you. Whether you use words, ideas, or images—or all three—is not important. Interact with God as one who loves and accepts you. Give to Him any discoveries you have during your experience.

- Rest in Jesus's embrace. When He invites you to return to your contemplation of His Word or to your inner dialogue with Him, do so. Learn to use words when words are helpful and to let go of words when they no longer are necessary. Rejoice in the knowledge that Jesus is with you in both words and silence. It's not necessary to anxiously assess the quality of your Lectio Divina experience, as if you were performing for God. The goal is to simply stay in the presence of God by praying through His Word.

- Consider journaling. Bring your journal to a friend or a ministry leader so you can share what you've been learning or ask questions about passages that are hard to understand.

4. Be present to others. When we listen to understand others rather than listen to build our case for responding to them, we honor their presence and their made-in-the-image-of-God beauty. And, in turn, our commitment to be present to others draws us out of the over-focus on our interior life that often fuels the downward spiral of depression. Besides your focused attention on them (maintaining eye contact, shunting aside distractions, and repeating back what you hear them say), follow this game-plan:

- When it comes to the choices that others are making in life, ask far more "why" questions than you typically would and make fewer pronouncements and prescriptions.
- When you pray with or for someone, stop first to ask Jesus how to pray before you open your mouth, then wait until you feel nudged in a particular direction. "Trust in the Lord with all your heart. And do not lean on your own understanding" (Proverbs 3:5).
- When others are struggling to understand something, resist the urge to be their "answer person"— instead, ask questions that force them to wrestle it out first.
- Stop long enough to consider how you're experiencing others, then describe the reflections of God's glory you see in them: "You have shown remarkable courage in facing your difficult family situation."

Once you begin to uncover the below-surface truth about someone, ask questions that plant seeds. Jesus did this with the woman at the well in John 4. Then make some educated guesses about how things work in this person's own "kingdom culture," helping them:

- Wrestle with truth about their life
- Reflect on their own trajectory

- See themselves the way God sees them
- Relax and open themselves to beauty

After a day-long solo retreat with a group of men who traveled to the retreat location together but spent the rest of the day apart, I (Rick) asked a man I didn't know well what his "takeaway" from the day was. His report seemed strangely vague to me and seemed to subtly reference a complaint about someone in his life. He seemed satisfied with his response, but I felt compelled to invite a deeper conversation. So I asked: "It seems like you're talking about a specific incident—what is it, and why did it come up today?" My question communicated to this man: *I'm listening with my whole self, and I'd like to know more.* When we stay fully engaged with the person and with the Spirit of Jesus, we speak or stay silent as we are prompted.

The great English poet Elizabeth Barrett Browning wrote:

Earth's crammed with heaven.
And every common bush afire with God;
But only he who sees takes off his shoes;
The rest sit round it and pluck blackberries.

When we're becoming more mindful, we're learning to slow down and pay eccentric attention to the nuances of our world and others—and to the nudges of Jesus—and then embracing their implications. This way of living beats back the noisy, bullying intrusions of our destructive narratives and makes us more aware of both our present needs and our present grace. We see "every common bush afire with God" in ourselves and in others. And we are determined to live with our shoes off—to receive the "blackberries" of grace that await us in the present moment.

WHAT YOU CAN DO IF . . .

You're the One Who's Struggling	You Care for Someone Who's Struggling
• At the beginning of your day, pause to thank God for something that happened the previous day. At dinnertime, pause to thank God for something that happened during the day. At bedtime, pause to thank God for something that will happen in the week to come.	• Invite your friend or loved one to do something physical with you—a class at a health club, a chore around the house, an outdoor project, a run in the park, a bike ride, playing musical instruments together, or a hike on a trail. Physicality keeps us anchored in the present.
• Look around your home and let your eye rest on a decoration—an object or a painting/print or a plant. Slow your breathing a little and simply appreciate why you decided to display that decoration; remember its meaning to you.	• When you're with your friend or loved one, pause often to ask: "Do you see that? Do you hear that? Do you smell that? Can you feel that? Do you taste this?" Each time, describe what you see or hear or smell or taste or touch, inviting your loved one to do the same.
• Follow the "steps" to practice Lectio Divina as you read Scripture.	• Share the practice of Lectio Divina with your friend or loved one.

- The next time a friend or loved one shares a struggle or a challenge with you, offer to pray for them—do it in a "dependent" way, by asking Jesus first how to pray. This will focus your attention away from yourself and onto your friend and Jesus.

- Be vulnerable with your friend or loved one and share your fears or anxieties or challenges—ask for prayer. Communicate that you need their support and love and friendship. Remember to voice (specifically) what you enjoy about him or her.

CHAPTER 9

CHANGING OUR INTERIOR NARRATIVE

How to Tell a Better (and Truer) Story about Who We Really Are by Determining and Continually Refining Our Organizing Principle

Taleesha* is battling a killer self-narrative fueled by the trauma she experienced as a child growing up in an overtly and covertly abusive home. She emerged into adulthood from that home with a firm belief that there was something fundamentally broken and wrong about her—like a weed planted deep in her soul had spread its roots around her true identity, slowly choking it to death. After six months of isolation and struggle during the COVID-19 pandemic, she wrote this in her journal:

> [That weed] is telling me that the pandemic is sadder and harder on me and my family because there is something wrong with me, and I deserve to have it harder—because I'm not as healthy as others are. That's it. It's a punishing attitude; and I deserve punishment because I'm not as healthy as my other friends. This is a lie, I know. And it's been growing ever since the pandemic started. The message of the lie is telling me that I've made it harder on my family

because I'm not as healthy or as capable or "on top of things" as the rest of my family and friends. It's a hard, judging, punishing lie. And it's always talking to me. It has no compassion, love, or mercy. And when I'm with others who remind me of my family, they seem to embody this lie in my life. There is something cold, uncompassionate, and uncaring in their responses to me....

The story we're telling ourselves about ourselves (our self-narrative) is always on the hunt for evidence and experiences that validate our foundational belief system, or "organizing principle" (OP). We've previously touched on core beliefs when we focused on schemas in Chapter Three. Remember, a schema is a cognitive framework that helps us organize and interpret information. They help us build our personal storylines. Our schemas are reinforced by cognitive distortions, which are consistent errors in logic that contribute to false conclusions and skewed perceptions of situations and interactions. Cognitive distortions are the result of biased information processing—we look for evidence that confirms our schemas and ignore evidence that rejects them. Schemas can become increasingly rigid and difficult to modify as people grow older.

Acclaimed writer David Foster Wallace, a suicide victim himself, writes in *Infinite Jest*:

The so-called "psychotically depressed" person who tries to kill herself doesn't do so out of quote "hopelessness" or any abstract conviction that life's assets and debits do not square. And surely not because death seems suddenly appealing. The person in whom Its invisible agony reaches a certain unendurable level will kill herself the same way a trapped person will eventually jump from the window of a burning high-rise. Make no mistake about people who leap from burning windows. Their terror of falling from a great height is still just as great as it would be for you or me standing speculatively at the same window just checking out the view; i.e. the fear of falling remains a constant. The variable here is the other terror, the fire's flames: when the flames get close enough, falling to death becomes the slightly less terrible of two terrors. It's not desiring the fall; it's terror of the flames. And yet nobody down on the sidewalk, looking up and yelling "Don't!" and "Hang on!" can understand the jump. Not really. You'd have to have personally been trapped and felt flames to really understand a terror way beyond falling.[1]

As Wallace suggests, the terror of unendurable depressive pain produces a feeling of "Trapped," which is shaped by the unhealthy OP "I Cannot Be Saved." But the way out of that pain, according to this unhealthy OP, is a deceit.

Identifying and modifying our cognitive distortions (debugging our code) is fundamental to recovery from a slide into suicidality. Even more foundational is determining our OP. We all have an OP that is influenced by our faith, family, relationships, society, experiences, and schemas—and it's reinforced by our cognitive distortions. And we can inadvertently live by an OP that does not fully match our aspirations, calling, or best interests. Living by our "default" OP is like pushing our boat into a river's current and floating wherever it takes us. In contrast, we can take intentional steps to build an OP that matches the way we want to live. A healthy OP is proactive and acts like a company's mission statement. It speaks to our value, the value of others, and our resilience, passions, and purpose.

We often use our religious beliefs or a faith practice to help us determine our OP. They help answer why we exist, what to expect in life, what's expected of us, what we do when we need help, and what promises we can expect to be kept: "I am created by an all-powerful God who loves me and has a plan for me." But we typically give little scrutiny to our OP, and hardly ever assess whether the framework it gives us has been infected by a software bug: "Yes, I am created by an all-powerful God who loves me and has a plan for me, but I must prove I am worthy." If you believe you are broken and useless and a source of pain for others, you become a magnet for attracting "corroborating storylines" that support and confirm your flawed OP. And catch the insidious hook that a deceptive OP tries to plant in your soul: "I deserve punishment because I'm not as healthy as my other friends."

Because our organizing principle is the lens through which we see all of life, it's crucial that we pay attention to it—a healthy, Jesus-centered OP is a bulwark against our descent into suicidality, while an unhealthy OP (fueled by our maladaptive schemas and further influenced by our cognitive distortions) will drive us deeper into it. We develop our OP over time (and all of us have one), even though we're often unaware of it. When I (Daniel) was grinding through my medical school rotations and dealing with relationship problems, my life was very challenging—I had lost my joy and my confidence and felt overwhelmed. I needed a place to stand, to "walk on water" just as Peter did when he responded to Jesus's invitation and climbed over the side of his boat. But, like Peter, I lost my resolve in the face of the threatening waves confronting me. I had come to believe that I had to do it all on my own. So I started marking Scripture passages in my Bible that reminded me of the truth. I read through these passages every night before I went to sleep, desperate to find my footing and longing for the strength to persevere. Over time, this practice built strength in me; it helped me to keep moving forward in the midst of my challenges. Because I was marinating in these truths every day, they began to shape in me an OP defined by the truths Jesus has revealed about me: I am more than a conqueror through Him (Romans 8:37). I can do all things through Christ who strengthens me

(Philippians 4:13). God's power is made perfect in my weakness (2 Corinthians 12:9), not the deceptions my experiences, schemas, and cognitive distortions were insinuating.

After the death of Moses, God spoke directly to his successor, Joshua: "Don't for a minute let this Book of The Revelation be out of mind. Ponder and meditate on it day and night, making sure you practice everything written in it. Then you'll get where you're going; then you'll succeed" (Joshua 1:8–10 TM). Our way forward is to marinate on the truth about God and (therefore) the truth about ourselves, over and over until our "default" OP retreats into the shadows, giving way to an OP built on our true Foundation.

Suicidality can develop out of our spiraling narratives when we become convinced, like Taleesha, that others' punishment for our "wrongness" isn't enough—that we will need to take charge of the punishment ourselves. This is an OP dictated by "Judgment [that] Demands Punishment" (to use palliative care expert David Kessler's term). For those who attempt suicide, the "sentence" for the "crime" of their existence is capital punishment—a death sentence. The Bible describes the enemy of God as a deceiver masquerading as an "angel of light" (2 Corinthians 11:14). For those who are struggling to beat back the darkness encroaching upon their soul, the deceit of capital punishment presents itself as a "fair sentence," given the "criminality" of their identity.

Pain raises the alarm in us—*it is not well with my soul*—but just as those who hear the shriek of a fire alarm know they need to escape but can't find the path to safety, we need a lighted escape route into freedom. Without it, the encroaching flames drive us to choose what feels like the lesser of two terrible fates. God is in the business of building fire escapes in our life. Our strongest defense in the face of the threats posed by our "infected" OPs, and the deceit that spawns them, is to find a new Narrator who will tell a better (and truer) story in our life. But we have spent many years investing our trust in the narrator of our twisted OP, and we don't leave behind trusted habits easily.

Here we offer three "lighted paths" that lead away from deceit and toward the truth. Follow them into a new Organizing Principle that is crafted and narrated by the same Guide who planted a redemptive story in the heart of the prodigal:

> While he was still a long way off, his father saw him coming. Filled with love and compassion, he ran to his son, embraced him, and kissed him. His son said to him, "Father, I have sinned against both heaven and you, and I am no longer worthy of being called your son." But his father said to the servants, "Quick! Bring the finest robe in the house and put it on him. Get a ring for his finger and sandals for his feet. And kill the calf we have been fattening. We must celebrate with a feast, for this son of mine was dead and has now returned to life. He was lost, but now he is found." So the party began. (Luke 15:20–24)

The prodigal son's OP had been "My Value Is in My Worldly Possessions," which his father corrected to "Your Value Is in Your Inherent Sonship."

1. **Reassert control over your story.** In a study published in the journal *Frontiers in Behavioral Neuroscience*, researchers explored why some childhood traumas become a source of resilience in adulthood, while other traumas lead to a victim mindset. "One of these factors," conclude the researchers, "is the degree of control that the person has over the stressor. Episodes of early uncontrollable stress can lead to 'learned helplessness,' where a person is conditioned to believe that they are unable to change the circumstances of their situation. Learned helplessness is also used as a model for depression in animals. When administered inescapable and erratic shocks, animals tend to develop heightened anxiety states and fear responses. These

dysregulations are likely to have severe negative repercussions on both cognition and mood."²

When we can't exert any control over the trauma we've experienced, the "agency" that fuels our hope is obliterated. Put another way, painful experiences that are "inescapable and erratic" can cut the soul's "tendons," making it difficult to use or strengthen the muscles we need to face and overcome future challenges and pain. The healing we need is directly tied to our ability to reassert control over our story—to reattach those cut tendons and rehabilitate our agency. This is not a rhetorical exercise; we need actual new experiences of exerting normal control over the outcome of our everyday challenges.

My (Rick's) friend Barry* has had a long history of cascading health concerns—one after another, all his life. He's also a victim of child sexual abuse, perpetrated more than once when he was just a toddler. Because of his age at the time of the abuse, Barry's trauma was "inescapable and erratic." Could his sometimes-overwhelming health concerns, including lupus (a chronic autoimmune disorder), heart problems, and a wide variety of lesser ailments, somehow be tied to the abuse he experienced when he was too young to understand what was happening to him and too little to offer real resistance? The trauma-body connection is well-researched and commonly accepted in the medical community. Canadian physician and trauma specialist Gabor Maté says: "Psychological influences make a decisive biological contribution to the onset of malignant disease through the interconnections linking the components of the body's stress apparatus: the nerves, the hormonal glands, the immune system and the brain center where emotions are perceived and processed."³

In his adult life, Barry sometimes experiences challenges and hurts that map to "inescapable and erratic." His response is almost always fueled by panic, tied to the destructive narrative of his abuse. In those moments control and agency drain out of him, and he retreats into a toddler's reality.

For example, when Barry's follow-up care was transferred to a new medical administrator who turned out to be incompetent, combative, and even deceitful, his breathing shortened, his eyes widened with fear, and his body tensed. He behaved like a man being chased down by a tiger. Barry called to tell me the story of his encounters with this person who was now in charge of making sure he received his prescriptions and care in an accurate, timely way—he reiterated every detail as if he were recounting a crime scene. I could tell he was gripped with terror. "I can't stand this feeling," he said. "I feel like I should just go down to that office and find someone in charge who can listen to my story and do something about it. But maybe I'm overreacting. Do you think I'm overreacting?"

"No," I responded, "I think that's a great idea. I think it's important for you to assert some control in this situation. I'll go with you if that would be a help." And so I picked up Barry from his apartment, and we drove to the medical office. He asked for a supervisor, and we went to a private room where Barry told the whole story in detail. As the supervisor expressed shock, concern, and a determination to intervene in the situation and stop the abusive behavior, Barry slowly descended from a "Defcon 1" defensive posture and relaxed his body and his breathing. The supervisor promised to confront the administrator the next day and take action.

On the way back from the encounter, Barry peppered me with questions about his behavior during the meeting, asking me repeatedly if he'd been appropriate or "over the top." When we stopped in front of his apartment building, I said, "You did a really good job in there, Barry." He looked at me, incredulous. "Really? I don't know…"

So I said, "Barry, why don't you tell yourself, out loud, 'I did a good job!'?" And he said, "I've never said those words to myself in my whole life."

I asked him to take a risk and say something to himself that sounded impossible and strange. When he resisted, I gently goaded him. Finally, he said it. It was weak at first, but as I prompted him to repeat it, he grew in conviction. After the fifth time repeating "I did a good job," he added an exclamation mark at the end.

This experience might seem insignificant, but it's actually a crucial step along the way in Barry's path back from an "inescapable and erratic" violation—new experiences of agency and control mesh well with the true story his Trusted Guide is trying to tell in his life: *You are strong. You can affect change with your actions. You are loved. You are defended. You are precious to Me. I will never leave you or forsake you. Keep going—don't give up.*

The idea is to exert what control and agency we can over difficult challenges, no matter how small or insignificant, as often as we can. We tell ourselves a different story—a story co-written by Jesus specifically to counter our destructive narratives—when we act on our God-given freedom to affect change in our environment. The goal is to build up a "story bank" of courageous acts in the face of what seems to be "inescapable and erratic." Essentially, we're disproving the deceit of our destructive narrative with a growing history of stories that spotlight our brave, consistent agency in the face of challenges. We are not doing this by sheer force of will; we are simply agreeing with the story Jesus is telling in our life and adding our "amen" to it by doing something that runs counter to the deceit we've so far accepted because it was, at one time, necessary for our survival.

2. **Broaden your perspective from telephoto to wide-angle.** Destructive narratives are pushy; they pester us to drill down and down into our psychological muck, promising to relieve the dissonance we experience in life with plausible distortions of the truth. Like a cow chewing its cud, we chew into the deceits we've embraced until we consume them, and they consume us. When this repetitive cycle kicks in, our "soul environment" is ripe for growing depression and suicidality—we need to be "knocked off our donkey." The Apostle Paul discovered the

blunt force of Jesus's love for him after he was jolted out of his own killer narrative.

> Meanwhile, Saul was uttering threats with every breath and was eager to kill the Lord's followers. So he went to the high priest. He requested letters addressed to the synagogues in Damascus, asking for their cooperation in the arrest of any followers of the Way he found there. He wanted to bring them—both men and women—back to Jerusalem in chains. As he was approaching Damascus on this mission, a light from heaven suddenly shone down around him. He fell to the ground and heard a voice saying to him, "Saul! Saul! Why are you persecuting me?" "Who are you, lord?" Saul asked. And the voice replied, "I am Jesus, the one you are persecuting! Now get up and go into the city, and you will be told what you must do." (Acts 9:1–6)

After three agonizing days of blindness in Damascus, when Saul refused to eat or drink, Jesus sent an emissary (Ananias) to lay hands on him for healing: "Brother Saul, the Lord Jesus, who appeared to you on the road, has sent me so that you might regain your sight and be filled with the Holy Spirit" (Acts 9:17). The effect of this traumatic experience stopped Saul's narrative "disease progression" and propelled him out of the psychological rut that had made him "utter threats with every breath." His crisis, followed by his healing, served to pull back his perspective, helping him see for the first time how the "pieces of the puzzle" fit together into a beautiful story of redemption that was planned and authored by the Trinity. As he understood and embraced the truth about Jesus, he began to explore his own role in the broader story Jesus was trying to tell in his life: "Saul stayed with the believers in Damascus for a few days. And immediately he began preaching about Jesus in the synagogues, saying, 'He is indeed the Son of God!'" (Acts 9:19–20).

The dynamic at work here is the result of creating distance from the belabored and rutted details of our destructive self-stories so we can see and embrace the broader story of our redemption from the perspective of Jesus. Author and church planter Aubrey Sampson calls this "the louder song," when God acknowledges the details of our reality but overshadows them with a perspective that helps us "taste and see" His goodness and beauty: "In a world full of hate, abuse, and game change," she writes, "God doesn't avoid or ignore pain. He sings a louder song over it. And he invites his hurting people to sing with him."[4] This is a healing invitation, but how do we practically respond to it?

In a *New York Times* op-ed, columnist David Brooks writes: "Think of one of those Chuck Close self-portraits. The face takes up the entire image. You can see every pore. Some people try to introspect like that. But others see themselves in broader landscapes, in the context of longer narratives about forgiveness, or redemption or setback and ascent."[5] Brooks is defining the difference between healthy introspection and unhealthy muck-drilling. Drawing from the work of psychologists, Brooks concludes: "The self is something that can be seen more accurately from a distance than from close up. The more you can yank yourself away from your own intimacy with yourself, the more reliable your self-awareness is likely to be."[6]

To play this out in your everyday life, you might...

Consider your life story through the lens of "the hero's journey," the embedded narrative "code" in all adventure stories. Joseph Campbell, a professor of literature and renowned host of a widely viewed PBS series on myth, describes this archetypal path: "A hero ventures forth from the world of common day into a region of supernatural wonder: fabulous forces are there encountered and a decisive victory is won: the hero comes back from this mysterious adventure with the power to bestow boons on his fellow man."[7] Translated into short-hand, we see the sorrows and traumas of our journey as necessary foils to overcome, and when we do, we discover we have rich treasures to offer others. This "wide-angle" view of our life accounts for our dark twists and turns the same way a skilled novelist builds heroic charac-teristics into his/her protagonist—conflict and heartbreak are neces-sary for the protagonist to emerge into "the truth of their being."

Seen this way, the pain that has produced our destructive narratives is a catalyst for our "becoming," not a verdict on our worth or value or essence. Jesus has a louder song He wants to sing over us.

As Jesus was walking along, he saw a man who had been blind from birth. "Rabbi," his disciples asked him, "why was this man born blind? Was it because of his own sins or his parents' sins?" "It was not because of his sins or his parents' sins," Jesus answered. "This happened so the power of God could be seen in him." (John 9:1–3)

Invite a trusted, insightful, and Jesus-dependent friend or counselor to help you re-narrate your story. We are created by God to find our identity outside of ourselves. That may sound like the very thing we've been told to avoid: "Don't let your career or your accomplishments or others' opinions of you define who you are." But we are created by God to discover the truth about ourselves by looking out, not in. Our friends, enemies, family, media, coworkers, spouse, siblings, and children all contribute to our "identity formation." Obviously, the story these out-side narrators are telling about us is a mix of truth and deceit and ignorance. But the story Jesus is telling us about ourselves has no impu-rity in it—no deceit. He's inviting us to give Him the freedom to sculpt our identity with the skills of a master artist. He wants His story about us to be our only comparable. And the way He re-narrates our story is most often through the reflection we invite from His "Body."

This may seem like an impossibly vulnerable step to take. That's why it's important to heed what Jesus says: "Don't waste what is holy on people who are unholy. Don't throw your pearls to pigs! They will trample the pearls, then turn and attack you" (Matthew 7:6). Chris Bruno says: "To tell someone else my story is tantamount to heart-level exposure that feels raw, naked, and risky. Yet, the more we become fluent in our stories, the more we settle into our own skin and recognize the greater purpose of our lives."[8] When we are caught in the downward draft of our self-stories, it's important to seek an outside perspective that can hear and ingest our "plot twists" and refashion the story Jesus is telling in our life.

To do this well, we need people who have already experienced the "re-narration" of their own story. A trained Christian counselor can help. In fact, while there are many skilled counselors and psychologists who do not follow Jesus (of course), a believer's re-narration must include the perspective of the Spirit, and only a follower of Jesus can offer that. When we find the right person, we narrate the story of our pain or heartbreak and offer it to our trusted "storyteller" as the raw material for reflecting back to us a new story, driven by the outside perspective of someone who is listening horizontally (to our story) and vertically (to the story Jesus is telling). The ancient African proverb is true: "People become people through other people."

Ask Jesus: "Who do you say I am?" After an exhausting season ministering to the crowds following Him, Jesus withdraws to a lonely place to pray with His disciples.

> He asked them, "Who do people say I am?" "Well," they replied, "some say John the Baptist, some say Elijah, and others say you are one of the other ancient prophets risen from the dead." Then he asked them, "But who do you say I am?" Peter replied, "You are the Messiah sent from God!" (Luke 9:18–20)

This question—"Who do you say I am?"—is vulnerable and risky. And Jesus is not hesitant to go first; a preamble to inviting us to do the same with Him. Soon after this interchange, He offers Peter a powerful reflection on his identity: "Now I say to you that you are Peter (which means 'rock'), and upon this rock I will build my church, and all the powers of hell will not conquer it" (Matthew 16:18). This will become Peter's new OP, as determined by Jesus. Like a child, we can follow Jesus's lead and simply ask Him to "mark the truth" about who we are.

Early in my (Rick's) marriage, after a season of escalating conflict with my wife, I left on a business trip and wrestled with the reality that divorce might be a real possibility. I was more than haunted by this—I was devastated, panicked, and desperate. I wanted God to reassure me that my worst fears would not come true, but He would not. Instead, as I sat on the floor in a darkened conference room far from home, pouring out my heart to Him, He confronted my distorted OP (that my soul was an empty place where something solid was supposed to be) by marking my true identity. As I scribbled what I "heard" on a legal pad, Jesus described my soul:

> *You're a quarterback. You see the field. You're squirming away from the rush to find space to release the ball. You never give up. You have courage in the face of ferocity—in fact, ferocity draws out your courage. You want to score even when the team is too far behind for it to matter. You love the thrill of creating a play in the huddle, under pressure, and spreading the ball around to everyone on the team. You have no greater feeling than throwing the ball hard to a spot and watching the receiver get to it without breaking stride. In fact, you love it most when the receiver is closely covered, and it takes a perfect throw to get it to him. You have the same feeling when you throw a bomb and watch the receiver run under it, or when you tear away*

*from the grasp of a defender, or when you see and feel
blood on your elbows or knees and feel alive because of it.
You love to score right after the other team has scored, but
you want to do it methodically, first down by first down,
right down the field. You love fourth down! You want to
win but are satisfied by fighting well.*

Oswald Chambers says, "God does not tell you what He is going
to do; He reveals to you Who He is."[9] Also, He is revealing who we
are. Jesus is far more interested in naming us than fixing all of our
challenging circumstances. When He named me "Quarterback," he
was giving me the one thing I needed to continue slogging through my
"valley of the shadow of death" and emerge out of the darkness on
the valley's rim, strengthened by an organizing principle authored and
influenced by truth, not deceit.

To pursue this "naming" experience in your life, you'll need a quiet
space where you're guaranteed privacy and uninterrupted time. A basement or bathroom or prayer room at your church are possibilities. Bring
something to write on and with. Your mission is simple: Ask Jesus,
"Who do you say that I am?" Then wait in silence for Him to respond.
Honor and receive what you "hear" by writing it down. Before you enter
this time, it's important to assert the authority God has given you and
first silence your own voice, then silence the voice of God's enemy. Do
this formally and out loud. Then, in the quiet, simply ask Jesus: "Who
do you say I am?" Wait in silence, relaxed and unconcerned about producing anything during this time. Imagine yourself as a catcher's mitt,
just waiting to receive whatever Jesus throws at you. It could be a word,
a phrase, a picture of something in your mind, a Scripture passage, or
a full-on description. It's possible you may not sense anything, and that's
(of course) okay—it's not a test of your spiritual maturity. Just ask like
a child, wait like a child, and respond like a child. If you get nothing,
smile and tell Jesus you'll return to the question another day.

If you do sense Jesus "marking" who you are, write it down, then consider who you can share this with. Ask your trusted person to mull over what you've shared and offer perspective or affirmation or even any "course correction" that might be needed. This is the purpose of the Body of Christ in our life—to affirm what Jesus is saying and doing in our story.

Asking Jesus to define who we are is not a one-time practice—it's an everyday habit. Instead of trying to argue our way out of dark places, we simply ask Jesus to re-narrate our story for us. Who do you say I am right now, Jesus? And we do this as often as we need to, until the truth of our identity, spoken over us by the Spirit of Jesus, begins to drown out the noisy, clamoring lies that our destructive narratives have produced.

3. **Nurture a push-back thought life.** It may sound strange, but when Jesus declares, "I must preach the Good News of the Kingdom of God" (Luke 4:43), He is also inviting us to enter His school of the martial arts—His "*dojo.*" In the martial arts, we learn to use the momentum of our enemy and redirect it in our favor. It's the skill of defusing the assault of what seems to be a much larger attacker by using the force of that attacker against him. And this is the problem facing the Trinity: the "much larger attacker" of humanity is separation from God through death, the consequence of our original sin. And the grace won by His sacrifice on the cross is the redirection of the assault into redemption.

In the martial arts, one strategy emphasizes a "hard" approach—match violence with violence. But the second strategy is "soft," and it is more shrewd, more Jesus-y: "The goal of the soft technique is deflecting the attacker's force to his or her disadvantage, with the defender exerting minimal force and requiring minimal strength."[10] If we consider our twisted schemas and distorted narratives (the natural consequences of our brokenness) as the attackers they are, then perhaps we can learn from Jesus how to counter their influence in our thought life, redirecting their force using strategies that reflect the soft technique of the martial arts.

We see God practicing this soft technique in the life of Joseph. After the envy and cruelty of his brothers, who sell him to slave traders and lie to their father about his fate, Joseph confronts them with the truth. They are desperate and needy now, because a famine has spread across the world, and only Egypt (because of Joseph's prophetic leadership) has the food reserves to survive it. So the brothers come to Egypt to beg for help, at first unaware that their fate is in the hands of the brother they left for dead. When Joseph reveals himself, the brothers (naturally) fear for their lives, especially for what would happen after their father, Jacob, died. But Joseph tells them:

> Don't be afraid of me. Am I God, that I can punish you? You intended to harm me, but God intended it all for good. He brought me to this position so I could save the lives of many people. No, don't be afraid. I will continue to take care of you and your children. (Genesis 50:19–21)

Joseph's OP would've included "Even Personal Pain Can Be Redeemed for Good." Here he is relating more than his own experience of God—he is describing a martial-arts pattern in the way God relates to all of us. God will take what is intended to harm us and redirect its momentum into a life-giving, redemptive outcome. But we have to bring Him the harmful thing in our life—the destructive momentum of our self-narrative—so He can "reapply" the force of it to bless instead of curse. Jesus is inviting us to give Him the raw material of our pain; He won't waste the impact of that pain if we actually give it to Him to work with. He will then take the momentum of our shattered life and treat it as clay, the medium He'll use to fashion a new work of art. He is a martial artist. And here is how we can partner with Him in this work:

"Out" your self-narratives. It seems counterintuitive, but we can use the force of our negative self-stories against them when we set free our interior dialogue from its captivity inside our soul. When we keep those looping narratives inside, they are like bulls in a locked china shop—they smash around our soul, wreaking havoc. But when we open the door to let those bulls out, their impact can be dispersed and even negated by the larger community.

I (Rick) have a friend who experienced debilitating trauma when he was young and was having great trouble overcoming the narrative seeds planted in his soul as a result. His counselor advised him to start telling his story to those in his close Christian community, but he resisted at first: "My counselor at the time was encouraging me to share my story of abuse with others, but I was reluctant because it seemed like asking a lot of those around me to 'carry the weight' of that story. My counselor reminded me that part of the calling of true community is to bear the burden of one another's stories. It was trans-formative for me to realize I needed my community to help me bear my story, just as they needed me to help them bear theirs."

Clinical psychologist Todd Essig adds: "Introspection is a closed system. Patterns of growth only emerge by opening yourself to input from others. Can you imagine doing a search on an iPhone with no network connection? Even the best search strategy, i.e., introspection alone, would be terribly limited. So too with cognition, feeling, and desire."[11] We who represent the "network connection" (the Body of Christ) to those whose interior narratives hold killer intent can "be Jesus" to them by asking questions that might seem like "prying" to our risk-averse sensibilities. I (Rick) often ask people lots of follow-up questions about their story, using cues from what they share to take the conversation deeper. When I explain to others what I do, their first response is that I must get a lot of awkward, push-back responses. But the opposite is true—most people are so starved for someone who will pursue their story as if they actually care about it that I've never, ever had someone balk at my pursuit.

Learn to question your self-narratives. Jesus, who physically left the earth so that the Spirit of Truth could enter our hearts and influence us from the inside out, plants in us a love for truth in all its forms. We can join the Spirit's work in our life by questioning the "givens" of our interior narratives, using the force of their arguments to expose their weak foundation. That means we ask ourselves questions like these:

- *Is this true in light of what I know about Jesus?* (Is this the sort of way Jesus would really talk or act? Can I imagine Jesus urging people to get on board with this?)
- *Is this a truth universally embraced by the Body of Christ?* (Jesus insists on a diversity of gifts and perspectives in his "Body," so how would a "foot" or a "hand" or an "eye" weigh in on this truth?)
- *Is it biblically true?* (Is this truth consistent with what Jesus says and does in the gospel accounts of His life, and is it congruent with the "meta-narrative" of the Bible's message?)
- *Is it true based on what I already know is true about the Kingdom of God?* (Jesus told parables to help us understand how things work in the Kingdom of God, so does this truth fit with what his parables have already revealed, or would it violate something Jesus has already made clear?)
- *Is it true on the face of it?* (If I scratch the surface of this truth, do I find a well-anchored foundation or a thin veneer under it? How quickly does it fall apart under closer scrutiny?)

- *Is the source of this truth healthy and Jesus-centered, or does it come from a distorted, unreliable source?* (Is this truth obviously serving a twisted, damaged, or pre-determined agenda?)
- *Is it the full truth, or does it represent only disconnected snippets of truth?* (What has been left out, accidentally or on purpose, in the description or context of this truth?)
- *Is it a culturally bent truth that serves a self-centered agenda?* (Is it a truth that makes sense no matter where I come from, or has it been reconfigured to support a narrow cultural perspective?)

Push back on your self-narratives by labeling them, then releasing them. Because our organizing principle leads our interior conversation, the themes and "catchphrases" of our soul don't change all that much without intentionality. Most of us are familiar enough with these narrative patterns that we can actually give them shorthand labels. For example:

- *A "Victim" OP might generate this thought:* "This world is out to get me. That person's random comment was meant to hurt me." Label: That's my Personal-Attack story.
- *A "Clueless" OP might generate this thought:* "I'm really just a Poser—I don't really know what I'm doing, so I fake it." Label: That's my Poser story.
- *A "Never Enough" OP might generate this thought:* "No matter how hard I try, or how much effort I throw at things, it never seems to be enough." Label: That's my Poverty story.
- *A "Try Harder to Be Better" OP might generate this thought:* "If I can just reach the goals that I've set for

myself, everything in my life will be okay." Label: That's my Overachiever story.

The idea is to get in touch with the common way you deal with struggles or hurts or disappointments in your life, identify the story you tell yourself, then give that story a label. Then, in the middle of that repetitive narrative cycle in your head, simply speak out that label, then treat it like a bird you've captured and let it fly away. Better yet, when you've identified the story and given it a label, ask Jesus to take it from you and release it "into the wild." Do this as often as you need to during your everyday life—there is no "acceptable limit" for the number of times you may need to repeat this "jailbreak" habit.

Redeem your self-narratives by defining your OP, or the mission of your life. We can launch a preemptive strike against the downward slide toward depression and suicidality by adopting an organizing principle that represents "the confident hope he has given to those He called" (Ephesians 1:18). Developing an organizing principle takes time and can morph and change right along with your own developing maturity, but it is not a passive process. That means it's important to write down your OP and the truths that undergird it so you can marinate on it until your soul is infused by it. Do this as often as you are able. This can be part of your daily devotion and daily prayer—calling on God to reveal His truths to you daily. This is especially important after labeling our unhealthy self-narratives, so we can avoid marinating in them.

Yes, Jesus will help us define our identity directly and indirectly through His Body, and He will "edit" our OP as we "put away childish things" (1 Corinthians 13:11). But this process will not have traction in our life until we write it all down. Consider this a quest to develop your personal mission statement—the purpose of your life, and the way you are determined to live with your relationship with Jesus at the center of it. It's a preemptive shift to living more intentionally, rather than drifting with the current of your default OP. For a helpful template you can use in your ongoing development of an OP, go to Appendix B on page 227.

WHAT YOU CAN DO IF...

You're the One Who's Struggling	You Care for Someone Who's Struggling
• Share your struggle with something that is out of your control with a trusted friend—together, brainstorm one simple way you can exert control over that situation, then do it.	• Offer to brainstorm with your friend or loved one a way to exert some level of control over something that has seemed out of their control. Gently invite your friend to try the best idea, then follow up.
• Think about your favorite "hero" story—from a book, a film, a song, a play, or a show. Ask yourself: In what ways has my journey been similar to the hero's journey in this story?	• Remind your friend or loved one about the "bigger picture" or "macro narrative" of their life—retell their story back to them, using the template of the hero's journey as a way of understanding the seemingly disparate circumstances of their life story.

• Pause, silence your voice, and take authority over the voice of God's enemy, then ask Jesus (simply): "Who do you say that I am?" Wait quietly, like a child, until you sense a response.	• Offer to pray on behalf of your friend or loved one. Simply silence your own voice, and the voice of God's enemy, and ask: "On behalf of _____, who do you say he/she is?" Then wait quietly, like a child, until you sense a response. Then share that response with your friend.
• Tell the story of your destructive narrative to a trusted friend—invite them to give you feedback about it.	• Ask your friend or loved one to share with you the narrative they've embraced about their life, then prayerfully and gently offer them your own "truth mirror" as a reflection on that narrative.
• Question the "givens" of your interior narrative using the list of questions on the previous pages.	• Give your friend or loved one a copy of the list of "push-back" questions about our interior narratives and explain how you have used those questions to "out" your own destructive narratives.
• Define your organizing principle by following the guidelines in Appendix B.	• Help your friend or loved one to define their organizing principle by giving him or her the guidelines in Appendix B.

CHAPTER 10

PLAY AS WARFARE

How We Find Our Way into "the Kingdom of the Child" and Then Live There

Logan is an eighteen-year-old freshman in college who is exploring the nooks and crannies of his new campus early in the morning before class begins:

> I had some time before my first class this morning, so I wandered around. And then the squirrels struck my curiosity. So I started watching and following them, just to kind of "play" with Jesus by asking Him to show me what the squirrels can teach me. And I got this out of it...
>
> We as humans are like the squirrels that roam campus—we are comfortable with anyone who is walking by as long as they are paying no attention to us. Yet it is ingrained in us that those who stop to pay attention are harmful. That's the nature of brokenness—the ones who stop are harmful. So we freeze. And then we find an escape if the person continues to pay attention. So it's no wonder we're afraid to walk

toward Jesus, the One who stopped, the One who notices
us when we shouldn't have been noticed...

Here Logan is slowing down to experiment and "play" in his
relationship with Jesus, allowing his creativity and intellect and imagination to reveal what is hiding in plain sight. At a stressful time in his
life—when he is far away from home for the first time and not yet
embedded in a new community of friends—this experiment in playful
intimacy with the One who will "never leave or forsake" him is a relief
and a source of strength. Because he is willing to stop in the midst of
his day to play on God's playground, to allow his soul to climb the
monkey bars and to pump his legs on the swing, he can face his new
challenges more wholly.

Toward the end of the great theologian and professor Dallas Willard's life, a former grad student asked him to describe Jesus with one
word. He chose "relaxed."[1] That is, Jesus not only urges us to play like
children if we hope to understand and embrace the Kingdom of God
(Luke 18:15–17), but He also models a relaxed and playful lifestyle. If
"playful" and "relaxed" seem like shocking descriptions of the stiff,
somber, intense Jesus we've often learned about in church, consider
this ridiculous "playground" story:

> On their arrival in Capernaum, the collectors of the Temple
> tax came to Peter and asked him, "Doesn't your teacher
> pay the Temple tax?" "Yes, he does," Peter replied. Then
> he went into the house. But before he had a chance to
> speak, Jesus asked him, "What do you think, Peter? Do
> kings tax their own people or the people they have con-
> quered?" "They tax the people they have conquered," Peter
> replied. "Well, then," Jesus said, "the citizens are free!
> However, we don't want to offend them, so go down to the
> lake and throw in a line. Open the mouth of the first fish

you catch, and you will find a large silver coin. Take it and pay the tax for both of us." (Matthew 17:24–27)

Here Jesus is responding with a playful attitude to a serious challenge to His integrity, delivered by the imposing "collectors of the Temple tax" (a fee levied for centuries on all men over twenty to pay for the upkeep of the Temple, or the "home" of God). Because He doesn't want to "offend" these men (a snarky, delightful comment coming from the same person who had no problem offending people at any the time), Jesus tells Peter to pay the men the same way David Blaine might if he was the Messiah: Find a four-drachma coin in the mouth of the first tilapia you catch? Is He Peter's "Rabboni" or a stand-up comedian? I'll be here all week, says the playful, relaxed Son of God.

When we meet the Jesus of the Bible, we're like children who've just arrived at the playground and found our best friend already on the swings. He wants us to "grow down" into childhood again. "Unless you are converted and become like children, you will not enter the Kingdom of Heaven" (Matthew 18:3 NASB).

Children at the time of Jesus were considered "beneath the dignity of reason"—they were seen as "fearful, weak, helpless, fragile, dependent, defenseless, and vulnerable." But Jesus destroys this conventional wisdom by elevating their trusting, joyous, playful, authentic, and all-in nature. When we grow down into childhood, we recapture the playful habits we once took for granted—creativity, emotional exuberance, risk-taking, experimentation, intellectual adventuring, community-building, and courage. And when we learn to live like children again, we experience the health and wholeness that defines the Kingdom of God. We blunt the edges of our destructive self-narratives.

In my clinical work with clients who are depressed or suicidal, I (Daniel) encourage them to nurture their creative outlets, engaging in the life activities that always make them feel good when they're doing them—to explore other outlets for emotional expression that are not (only) inward-facing. These are activities that my clients rarely see as important to their mental health. But they simply don't understand the serious power of fun—of childlike delight. And in Hosea 4:6, God grieves the impact of our ignorance: "My people are destroyed for lack of knowledge" (NASB). In the context of play and its redemptive power to slow the pull toward depression and suicidality, if we understood and embraced its important role in our overall brain health—if we learned to fuel creative expression in our life—then we could build a bulwark against the destruction that presses in on us.

It doesn't matter what our preferred form of play is as long as we enjoy it. If we feel good when we're doing something that requires creativity, then it's a path of grace Jesus has given to us. This means all creative outlets "work"—writing, photography, drawing, sculpting, carpentry, sewing, dancing, speaking, computer coding, gardening, event planning, making music, painting, filmmaking, cooking or baking, knitting, crafting poetry, acting, making pottery, journaling, teaching, playing board games, scrapbooking, and on and on. The Victorian-era newspaperman and apologist G. K. Chesterton says: "Mathematicians go mad, and cashiers; but creative artists very seldom. I am not...in any sense attacking logic: I only say that this danger does lie in logic, not in imagination."

The evidence for the "booster rocket" influence of play and creativity is overwhelming. We'll highlight eight examples here:

1. **Dance.** In a study that focused on dance movement therapy (DMT), a growing practice within the psychological community, "results suggest that DMT and dance are effective for increasing quality of life and decreasing clinical symptoms such as depression and anxiety."[2] In fact, when a cross-disciplinary team of health and performing-arts specialists studied all the available research into the impact of dance on even severe depression, they "report[ed] a drastic

improvement and a sharp shift from severe depression to mild depression." And one study's results showed that "body-movement intervention" through dance practices resulted in "minimal depression"—or "appearing to present full recovery."[3]

2. **Arts and Crafts.** In a group of adolescents suffering from posttraumatic stress disorder (PTSD), some were included in art therapy sessions, and some were not. Those who experienced this "intervention," say researchers, saw results that were "significantly better than [the] control [group] at reducing PTSD symptoms...."[4] And when researchers recruited college students to join an art-making group (painting, drawing, clay modeling) just one week before their final exams, they found huge decreases in their anxiety levels, compared to a control group.[5] Finally, in a study comparing the mood-improving impact of squeezing a stress ball versus molding a pinch-pot out of clay, researchers found "the clay work has specific efficacy for reducing negative mood states."[6]

3. **Photography.** When a group of researchers decided to explore the impact of the daily practice of photography, they recruited people who agreed to shoot and post at least one photo a day on a website built to display their work. They were encouraged to "narrate" their photos and interact with others on the site. The study concluded that the practice had a significant impact on feelings of well-being among those who participated.[7] After writer and photographer Danielle Hark fell into a deep post-partum depression and began struggling with suicidality, she reached for her phone to call for help during a panic attack and instead snapped a photo of a crack in her bathroom wall. Something about the stark beauty of that accidental photograph captured her, sparking a daily habit that helped to drag her out of the darkness. "Just that one thought and just that one breath helped me to become more present," she says.[8]

4. **Role-Playing Board Games.** For a college student battling suicidal depression, an accidental experience playing a complex,

multi-player narrative board game saved his life. "It's hard to express in words," he writes, "but after years of literally nothing less than constant, all-pervading mental agony, it meant so much to me to be able to...not feel that? To experience something good? The closest word I can find for it was 'love.' Giddy, goofy-grinning love, being unlocked from the black hole of my terrified mind by cardboard and plastic and rules, combining to connect me to the friends I had missed so very, very badly."[9] According to a study published in the journal *BioPsychoSocial Medicine*, playing board games "helps to improve cognitive impairment and depression."

Game-playing—the multi-player card game Bridge, for example—is a proven depression-fighter. One avid player, who's struggled with depression for many years, wrote this on a message board for Bridge enthusiasts: "Instead of doing things on your own, which makes it all too easy to 'lose interest,' you are constantly interacting with other people. This is something that certainly eases the effects of depression. If you play regularly, especially at a club, as I do, you have to keep on playing. Flouncing out would be letting down your partner, and that's an incentive to keep trying."

5. **Writing/Journaling.** Dragging our inside stories out into the light has profound therapeutic benefits. In a comprehensive review of the impact of art forms on mental and emotional health, researchers found that "individuals who have written about their own traumatic experiences exhibit statistically significant improvements in various measures of physical health," including depression, "negative mood," sleep disorders, and fatigue.[10]

6. **Music.** Music therapy programs are now common and popular in psychological circles, but much of their perceived impact has been anecdotal, since empirical research has been lean. But in a study of the available research, music therapy is a proven anxiety-reducer, calming neural activity in the brain and restoring active functioning in the immune system.[11] Apart from therapeutic approaches, just listening to

music in the midst of difficult seasons in life can have a profound impact. Researchers studying post-operative care strategies for people who experienced a serious heart attack found "reductions in heart rate, respiratory rate, myocardial oxygen demand, and anxiety after twenty minutes of relaxing music."[12]

It appears that active engagement in music, not just treating it as background ambience, is one key to its positive impact on depression and anxiety. This is why live music experiences can be a game-changer for people suffering from the after-effects of trauma: "You have to understand what it means for a combat veteran to be agitated in the waiting room," says Dr. Hani Khouzam, a staff psychiatrist at a California VA hospital that hires live musicians to play near its entrance. "Their pupils are dilated. They are angry or waiting for something to happen. But when we have live music that day, they come to me far more relaxed. It's like an amazing miracle, and I don't say that lightly."[13]

Finally, those who play music (not just listen to it) discover that it's a powerful brain-booster. "It engages every major part of the central nervous system," says John Dani, Ph.D., who is chair of neuroscience at the University of Pennsylvania's Perelman School of Medicine. "Recent studies suggest that music may be a uniquely good form of exercising your brain. Fun can also be good for you."

7. **Cooking and Baking.** During the COVID-19 pandemic, I (Rick) found myself volunteering to cook dinner several times a week, usually asking my family to let me prepare the entire meal alone, with jazz music playing loudly in the background. My wife has a lung disease brought on by an immune deficiency, so our household was in virtual lockdown for much of 2020. And I have two young-adult daughters who experienced a cascade of grief and loss as their schools shut down, their social life constricted, and everything they were looking forward to was wiped out. It was as if Thanos snapped his fingers and made

normal life disappear. Meanwhile, I had significant challenges to face in my work life and major transitions to navigate. I felt stress and anxiety and the downward pull toward depression. At the time I didn't understand exactly why I needed to cook so badly, but I did. Now, in retrospect, I know my soul was craving a creative, playful outlet that promised immediate feedback and results. My experience with this was both personal and universal.

In a "diary study" of more than six hundred volunteers who agreed to journal their daily experiences with creative outlets like cooking and baking, researchers discovered that those who participated in "more than normal" everyday creativity recorded a much higher "positive affect." The study's authors wrote: "These findings support the emerging emphasis on everyday creativity as a means of cultivating positive psychological functioning."[14] Melanie Denyer, founder of the Depressed Cake Shop, a bakery she uses to highlight mental-health awareness, says: "A lot of us turn to baking when we're feeling low. Some of us even started baking because they were ill and needed something simple as a focus. And there is genuinely something very therapeutic about baking."[15]

8. **Playing with Prayer.** As Logan modeled with his campus squirrel population, we've been invited by Jesus to relax more than we typically do in our relationship with Him. For example, we've been taught that prayer requires certain words, certain biblical maturity, and a certain tone. But none of that is true. When His disciples ask Jesus to teach them to pray, He knows they're looking for the "right formula." Instead, He gives them guidance on how to pray, not what to pray: "When you pray, don't babble on and on as the Gentiles do. They think their prayers are answered merely by repeating their words again and again. Don't be like them, for your Father knows exactly what you need even before you ask him! Pray like this: 'Our Father in heaven...'" (Matthew 6:7–9). The word translated "Father" here is the Greek word *Abba*, which is

better translated as "Daddy." It's a child's way of relating. Jesus is emphasizing a relaxed approach to prayer rather than the formulaic, outcome-based, and technical way we typically relate to Him. He begins His guidance by emphasizing the child's perspective, because play, as Maria Montessori famously said, "is the work of the child."

Here's how I (Rick) have been training people for decades to relax and play more in the way they relate to God. I call this approach "dependent prayer"—essentially, instead of assuming we already know what to pray for, we simply ask Jesus first for guidance. Our typical approach to prayer—whether for ourselves or when we're praying for others—is to consider what we need or what we hope for and then brainstorm our (somber-sounding) requests. In a more playful, dependent approach we:

1. First assert authority over and silence both our own "brainstorming" voice and the voice of God's enemy, Satan.
2. Ask Jesus for guidance in what and how to pray, then wait in silence.
3. Receive, like a child, whatever word, phrase, passage, or image pops into our head.
4. Then, asking Jesus for help, we pray, using the guidance He's given us.

Over the years I've seen thousands of people react with astonishment as their prayers for others, and others' prayers for them, playfully "hit the mark" in a way they've never experienced before. They realize in these moments that Jesus is not nearly as uptight as they assumed. And they are free to explore their relationship with Him creatively, imaginatively, and intimately. He wants us to join Him on the playground—He's been patiently waiting on the monkey bars for a long time.

WHAT YOU CAN DO IF...

You're the One Who's Struggling	You Care for Someone Who's Struggling
• If you love to dance, do your thing. If you hate to dance, do it in short spurts in safe spaces (think of it as bringing delight to others, who will not be expecting you to "break out" like this).	• Invite the person to a group dance class or venue that offers line dancing or other forms of group dance. If the person is in your home, play a little dance music every now and then and be spontaneous.
• Take a community-based craft class, or watch an instructional video on how to paint in watercolor or make your own flower pots. Make crafts as birthday or holiday gifts. If you keep a journal, draw your prayers instead of using words.	• Ask your friend or loved one to make something for you, if they are skilled in a craft. Take a community-based crafting class together.
• Take more photos with your camera pointing away from you, rather than toward you. Instead of conventional posed or scenic shots, think about taking some photos that could appear in a book of photography—use that imagined standard as a spark for creativity.	• Ask your friend or loved one to "document" a special event as your amateur photographer.

• If you have a family with children still at home, designate one weekend night as "Family Game Night." Play games that appeal to both younger and older players.	• Invite your friend or loved one to join your "Family Game Night" every now and then. Join on online role-playing game group with your friend. For fun, go to a game arcade together and play for an hour or so. Play "Words with Friends"—download the app from your phone's app store.
• Keep a journal—if this is not something you've done before, choose a small-format journal so you don't feel pressure to "fill up the page."	• With your friend or loved one, write "crowd-sourced" poetry together. Send a text with the first line of a poem, then your friend sends the next line, and so on until the poem seems finished.
• Every month find a place to listen to live music—you can search for free live music online.	• Invite your friend or loved one to listen to live music with you.
• Try a new recipe every other week, making something you've never made before.	• Ask your friend or loved one to join you to cook or bake something you can give to someone needy in your neighborhood or community.

• Practice dependent prayer—ask Jesus how to pray for your challenges and needs before you open your mouth.	• Practice dependent prayer with your friend or loved one—ask Jesus first how to pray for him or her, then pray.

CHAPTER 11

FIGHTING DARKNESS WITH LIGHT

Why Our Physical Environment Matters So Much and Eight Simple Ways to Impact Your Emotional Health by Changing Your Surroundings

About ten years ago, my (Rick's) wife gave me an ultimatum: It was time to (finally) paint our interior walls with a color something other than white. We bought our house, in part, because it had so many large windows, and that made our interior environment rich with light and natural colors from the outdoors. Frankly, I hadn't really thought about the color of our walls because the beauty spilling through our windows was so inviting and warm. (Also, I'm a guy.) But I knew my wife had been biding her time, eager to add some variety to our living spaces. Then she said something that made my blood chill: "I have a friend who told me she hired a 'colorist' to come assess their color preferences and make paint suggestions—she charges $90 an hour, but we'd probably only need two hours..." I think my jaw must have dropped, cartoon-style. Frankly, this sounded like something a Kardashian might do, not a Lawrence. The list of things we could spend $90 or $180 on scrolled through my brain, and it was an impressive catalog of essentials. I was in automatic-protest mode.

But you already know what happened next: I finally agreed to hire the colorist, but with a hard one-hour limit.

I was not happy, and I made sure my wife had no doubts about that. When the colorist arrived at our door, I was pleasant and welcoming and...tense. I counted the minutes the woman spent engaging us in polite banter. But then, like a jaguar stalking her prey, she set off to prowl our house, studying the colors we'd already chosen with our furniture and decorations and bed coverings. She had a flip deck of Pantone colors that she sorted through, trying out colors on basically every wall in our house. All of this took a very long time, and the thermometer level on my face spiked to red. Finally, she gave us her pronouncement—far past the hour limit I'd set. With small pieces of tape fixed to all our walls, she recommended that we use five different colors throughout the house, many of them simply a darker or lighter shade of the same color, and one of them a color so dark that I thought she was joking. At this point I could not escape this nightmare, so I did the only thing guaranteed to maintain peace in my relationship with my wife: I bought into the mad science of the colorist.

And so we painted our walls exactly as this woman had recommended, even when I couldn't conceive how this would work out well. But when it was all done, I stood back and looked at our home. It was stunning. Warm, inviting, magnetic, and deeply satisfying. The emotional and psychological boost these complementary colors gave me was palpable and still saturates me with restoration to this day.

I am now a colorist believer. It may be the only thing I have in common with the Kardashians.

Strategies for Environmental Therapy

Of course, we all want to be surrounded by environmental beauty, but the impact of our surroundings goes far past aesthetics. Colors, sounds, lighting, smells, and tactile experiences in our living environments can give us a "background" boost in our journey out of the valley of the shadow of death. Essentially, anything that helps us embrace a narrative of life, not death, is an important ally. And anything that supports or magnifies our twisted schemas or cognitive distortions is an enemy. E. Fuller Torrey is president of the Treatment Advocacy Center. His mission is to advance and innovate psychiatric strategies, and he's made "environmental health" a major focus of the Center. Columbia University Medical Center's Alan Brown, an associate professor of clinical psychiatry and epidemiology, is an avid supporter of that focus: "If environmental risk factors for [mental illness] can be validated and confirmed, there is every reason to expect they will point to preventive measures that lower their risks and morbidity."[1]

Our environment can promote or discourage social interactions—an inviting, safe, well-lit, and comfortable space tacitly invites people to slow down and enjoy each other and subtly encourages them to stay longer once they've made a connection. This kind of social support has a profound impact on well-being. Also, researchers know that brightly lit rooms (natural or artificial) influence positive outcomes with those who are facing depression, agitation, and sleeplessness. Conversely, a cluttered, smelly, and dirty environment prompts people to treat their surroundings with even more disrespect, and this can spill over into relational disrespect. In an atmosphere of disrespect, those who are struggling to overcome their destructive narratives have even more of an uphill climb.

It's important to remember that Jesus said, "consider the lilies of the field," "consider the sparrows," "consider the fig tree," "consider the seeds sown along the path," and on and on. He is always pointing us to our physical environment, urging us to pay focused attention to the lessons it is teaching us and its influence on our soul. Why does He do this? Because our surroundings matter. So here we explore ten environmentally connected strategies that can help us in our journey toward wholly living:

1. **Restorative Aromas.** Researchers pored over the results of six aromatherapy studies, looking for evidence that certain smells can impact the onset of depression, or help in our recovery from it. They found that some studies "showed positive effects of this intervention among these three groups of patients," and they recommended that aromatherapy be used as a "complementary and alternative therapy for patients with depression and secondary depressive symptoms arising from various types of chronic medical conditions."[2] Dr. Mason Turner, chief of psychiatry at Kaiser Permanente San Francisco, says, "Aromatherapy really can help bring a person into the present moment."[3]

Of our five senses, smell influences brain activity more than any other. Our "olfactory bulbs" are embedded in our limbic system, the area of the brain where we process emotion. "This is one of the reasons why so often something that we smell will trigger a memory or remind us of something or someone," says Beverley Hawkins, owner of the Vancouver-based West Coast Institute of Aromatherapy.[4] So:

• **Test the aromas of your shampoos, soaps, facial and hand creams, lip balms, and perfumes or colognes for their "mood effect."** Take a sniff, then immediately decide if the smell is pleasing or not. Some soap fragrances, for example, will make you immediately recoil, even a little. Some will make you immediately want a second sniff. Choose the "second-sniffers," because something about that aroma is soothing or mood-altering. Yes, we know this simple strategy seems like a no-brainer, but it's more truly a "health-brainer."

• **Drink chamomile tea, which is a proven "supplementary aid" for those struggling with depression.** It's a triple help because you're tasting and smelling and absorbing (feeling) the chamomile simultaneously.

• **Use the following (pure) essential oils as an ongoing therapeutic boost for your feelings of well-being:** jasmine, sandalwood, ylang-ylang, clary sage, basil, bergamot, rose, geranium, neroli, petitgrain, lavender, and chamomile. You can use a diffuser, a room spray, bath oils, a bowl of water with a few drops of oil, or massage oils to experience these pure scents.

2. **Color Therapy.** Just when you thought you'd heard all the pseudo-psychiatric expressions you can stomach, here's a new one: "chromotherapy." It's a centuries-old practice rooted in theories about how we "absorb" colors as human beings. The idea is that colors along the spectrum emit different electromagnetic energies which, in turn, can impact our physical and psychological health. If that sounds, well, sketchy, consider this description of chromotherapy from two alternative-medicine researchers:

> Chromotherapy is a narrow band in the cosmic electromagnetic energy spectrum, known to humankind as the visible color spectrum. It is composed of reds, greens, blues and their combined derivatives, producing the perceivable colors that fall between the ultraviolet and the infrared ranges of energy or vibrations. These visual colors with their unique wavelength and oscillations, when combined with a light source and selectively applied to impaired organs or life systems, provide the necessary healing energy required by the body. Light affects both the physical and etheric bodies. Colors generate electrical impulses and magnetic currents or fields of energy that are prime activators of the biochemical and hormonal processes in the human body, the stimulants or sedatives necessary to balance the entire system and its organs.[5]

Translated, this means that colors in our surroundings are having a deeper impact on our soul than we typically realize. The great twentieth-century philosopher Marshall McLuhan said: "Environments are not passive wrappings, but are rather, active processes which are invisible."⁶ He means that our physical surroundings, including colors, "wrap" us and are not passive—they are actively influencing us all the time, though in the background. In the world of chromotherapy, colors are tied to broad physical and psychological outcomes. The chart below covers the basics.

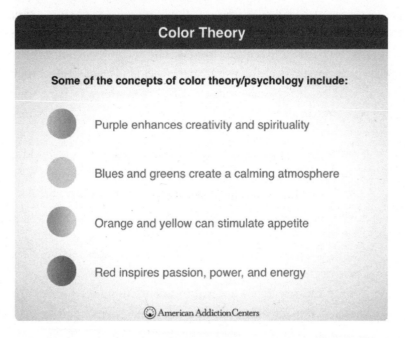

Color Theory

Some of the concepts of color theory/psychology include:

Purple enhances creativity and spirituality

Blues and greens create a calming atmosphere

Orange and yellow can stimulate appetite

Red inspires passion, power, and energy

American Addiction Centers

Drilling down a little, art therapists have made some broad assertions about the impact of "cool" and "warm" colors on our psychology (which, by the way, can change and morph according to cultural interpretations and norms):

• **Cool Colors.** Purple balances red and blue, which produces a mix between stimulation and calm. This translates into a prompt for creativity—the kind that can envision an alternate way out of our stuck-in-a-pothole reality. The lighter shades of purple are tied to peacefulness—the settled feeling you have when you see lavender, for example. Shades of green and blue translate to restfulness; green, in particular, is in the color bandwidth that focuses directly on the retina, making it less of a strain on our eye muscles. Blue slows our breathing and lowers our blood pressure, creating a sense of serenity. And researchers have discovered that shades of pink can significantly lower heightened states of aggression (toward others and toward ourselves): "Pink light has a tranquilizing and calming effect within minutes of exposure. It suppresses hostile, aggressive, and anxious behavior. Pink holding cells are now widely used to reduce violent and aggressive behavior among prisoners...."[7]

• **Warm Colors.** How much yellow and orange do you see in your favorite restaurant, or in the food advertising you see online or in your mailbox? Savvy restaurateurs and marketers use these "flame" colors to stimulate our appetite, because warm colors are stimulating (consider the color scheme in marketing and packaging for McDonald's, for example). So, when we feel stuck in the darkness, our soul craves light; muted colors will not invite us out of that place. But bright colors (especially yellow) reflect more light, and therefore pour more light into our thirsty soul.

These broad generalizations about color can influence our choices as we "curate" our surrounding environment, including:

- ○ Choosing which colors to paint or decorate your rooms, using color to complement (not hinder) your journey toward brain health.
- ○ Considering nature when you choose colors for your home and work surroundings—the brown of the earth, the green of the trees and grass, and the blue of the sky.
- ○ Finding ways to expose ourselves to the bright color spectrum either naturally (sunlight) or artificially (using light bulbs that replicate sunlight).

For a deeper look at colors and the impact associated with them, go to arttherapyblog.com and click on "Colors" at the top.

3. **Auditory Stimulation.** Much of the work and innovation around treating depression that leads to suicidality has focused on "top-down" approaches—therapies (including drug and psychiatric) that spotlight the "root of the tree" (the limbic area of the brain, in particular). These strategies target the central part of the brain with the goal of eventually reaching the "branches and leaves" of the tree (the way we experience and process our world through our five senses), and they have produced positive results for many. But some researchers are now questioning whether a "bottom-up" approach might also deliver brain- and mood-altering impact—therapies that enter through the portals of our five senses and carry restorative impact to the central areas of the brain that are suffering, "activat[ing] the same central affective neurocircuitry involved in depression...."[8]

We know that loud, continuous noise produces anxiety and depression. That's both anecdotally and scientifically true.[9] And people who are experiencing inner-ear disorders and deafness are also more likely to struggle with depression. Conversely, soothing, harmonic noise can reduce and regulate our anxiety and symptoms of depression. Sounds can heal, or they can hurt. So, here are a few possibilities for creating a healthy, restorative sound environment in your life:

• **Get your hearing checked.** Make an appointment with an audiologist to get your hearing checked. If there has been hearing loss, agree on a plan to compensate for it. Also, make an appointment with an ear, nose, and throat specialist (ENT) to have your inner ears cleaned of wax. Look for an ENT who uses video-guided soft scrapers, not one that "irrigates" your ears to remove the wax.

• **Listen to white noise when you're going to sleep.** White noise works by blunting the impact of sudden louder sounds, "averaging" the sound you hear to reduce the variations that startle your brain. It's produced by combining the sounds of all frequencies together into one "stew" of tones. You can find and purchase white-noise machines widely, but you can also use everyday white-noise emitters such as a fan or air purifier.

• **Listen to instrumental music for restoration.** Classical, instrumental jazz, meditation, and "New Age" music can all modulate your anxiety and bring a sense of calm. Three decades ago, Spain's Benedictine Monks of Santo Domingo de Silos released an album of medieval chant music that inexplicably vaulted to #3 on the Billboard pop charts, then spent fifty-three weeks there. Its popularity kicked off a tsunami of like-minded "ancient sacred" music, all infused with slow-flowing melody, monophonic in texture, with no harmony and no traditional rhythm. These elements combine to produce a relaxing, calming effect—pulling the listener into the present moment. In addition, studies show sad or "lament" music can help provide a pathway for grief that serves the grieving person like an "empathic friend."[10]

• **Listen to stimulating music to climb out of the valley.** For those looking to jolt themselves out of a depressive rut, rock (18 percent), alternative (10.6 percent), and pop (10.6 percent) are the top choices of more than 2,400 people surveyed by the Family Center for Recovery.[11] For a more comprehensive look at music styles and their impact on our emotions and psychology, go to fcfrmd.com and search for "Good Vibrations."

4. **Clean Air.** According to a research report published in the British newspaper the *Guardian*, "people living with air pollution have higher rates of depression and suicide.... Cutting air pollution around the world to the EU's legal limit could prevent millions of people becoming depressed, the research suggests." Isobel Braithwaite, the University College London professor who led the World Health Organization research team studying the impact of air quality on mental health, says: "We've shown that air pollution could be causing substantial harm to our mental health, making the case for cleaning up the air we breathe even more urgent.... We know that the finest particulates from dirty air can reach the brain via both the bloodstream and the nose,

and that air pollution has been implicated in increased [brain] inflammation, damage to nerve cells and to changes in stress hormone production, which have been linked to poor mental health." Another study found that growing up around "dirty air" quadruples a child's chance of developing depression later in life.[12]

The purer the air in your environment, the less likely you are to experience a "drag" on your psychological health. Impure air, according to researchers, actually leads to changes in brain structure.[13] So, a proactive approach to clean air means:

• **Stay inside, if possible, on "bad air" days.** It's easy to search for a local source for air quality index—just plug in your city name and "air quality" to a search engine (aqicn.org is a great choice). You should get an up-to-date index number that translates to "good," "moderate," "unhealthy for sensitive groups," "unhealthy," "very unhealthy," or "hazardous." If you live in an urban area, close your windows during morning and evening rush hours, no matter what the air quality level is that day.

• **Immerse yourself in fresh-air environments.** When weather permits and air quality is good, open your windows (if possible) to expose yourself to fresh air. Close your windows and use air conditioning or an air purifier or fan when the index number is moderate or higher. If possible, it's important to be outside for at least thirty minutes on good air days.

• **Wear pollution protection.** If you have to expose yourself to bad air quality, wear a HEPA-filter N95 mask to filter out all but 5 percent of pollution particles. N95 masks were in high demand during the COVID-19 pandemic, but they are also effective against poor air.

• **Cut sources of bad air in your indoor environments.** Tobacco smoke, which contains "fine and ultrafine" particulates, is a major source of indoor air pollution. That gray smoke is made up of four thousand chemicals in addition to the particulates. If you're struggling with depression or suicidality, tobacco smoke will make your journey out of the valley more difficult.

5. **Temperature Comfort.** Climate change is now a prominent topic in the news and in political/business circles. Its impact is far-reaching and long-term. But one overlooked impact is the role temperature change plays in mental health. In a data-mining study that compares rising temperatures to depression and suicidality rates, researchers say: "Our main estimates imply that increasing average monthly temperature by 1°F leads to a 0.48 percent increase in mental health [emergency department] visits and a 0.35 percent increase in suicides."[14] Sleep deprivation as a result of increasing temperatures is one key driver, according to the study's authors. They sum up with this: "Cold temperatures reduce negative mental health outcomes while hot temperatures increase them."[15] Unfortunately, the evidence suggests that human beings are very slow to adapt to rising temperature norms, leaving many struggling against a foe they can't control and can't see.

Of all the "natural disasters" that fuel our fears, heat is actually the top weather killer, causing far more deaths every year than any other—almost three times as many as tornadoes do. If we're going to prepare for the worst Mother Nature has to throw at us, our best investment is an air conditioner. In addition, follow these general guidelines:

• **Hydrate well.** Drink plenty of fluids, even if you're not thirsty. Experts say that translates to about 15.5 cups (3.7 liters) of fluids for men. And about 11.5 cups (2.7 liters) of fluids a day for women.

• **Avoid dehydrating liquids.** Alcohol, coffee, tea, and caffeinated soft drinks can actually diminish the heat-fighting impact of liquids. Consume moderate levels every day—one drink of alcohol a day for women and two for men, and two-to-four eight-ounce cups of coffee. (By the way, in a 2013 study published in *World Journal of Biological Psychiatry*, moderate caffeine consumption was linked to a reduction in suicide risk.)[16]

• **Dress light.** Wear loose-fitting, lightweight, and light-colored clothing, especially if you're outdoors in direct sunlight.

• **Don't overheat.** Limit your outdoor activity to morning and evening hours when it's cooler.

• **Use sunscreen.** Over-exposure to sunlight leading to sunburn can heat up your body, so use sunscreen whenever you plan to be outside in the sun for more than five minutes.

• **Eat light.** Heavy foods can impact the way your body regulates heat.

• **Get wet.** Use a damp cloth on your forehead or the back of your neck during hot parts of the day, or take a cool shower, jump in a swimming pool, or simply splash your face with cool water throughout the day.

6. The Truth about Feng Shui. Look around the home of a person struggling with suicidality and you're likely to see evidence of internal disorder leaking out into external disorder—signs of excess shopping, dusty and unclean surfaces, unmade beds, dark lighting, clutter, and "maintenance" issues such as dripping faucets, dying plants, or peeling paint. When life seems like a sinking slog through quicksand, there is no energy left over to keep up with normal chores and upkeep. And unkempt surroundings act like a self-fulfilling prophecy: the more the environment descends into chaos, the more the soul descends into chaos. It's possible to affect the trajectory of this spiral by addressing the orderliness of the home environment with strategies borrowed from feng shui philosophy.

Feng shui, or "wind-water" in Mandarin Chinese, is the art and science of object placement. In its Westernized form, practitioners use it to make interior decorating decisions. The idea is to reorder your living environments to produce a sense of "soul harmony" using decorations, objects, and furniture to create a more ordered and natural flow to your home or office architecture. Central to the strategy is a tool called a "bagua map," which divides the home or room into life-related zones, including wealth, health, relationships, career, and personal growth. This concept has been popularized on a massive scale—and simplified—by the success of Marie Kondo's runaway bestseller *The Life-Changing Magic of Tidying Up*. Kondo's approach is to declutter living environments by keeping only those things that "spark joy" and getting rid of anything that doesn't.

How does any of this jibe with the Kingdom-of-God norms Jesus promoted and modeled? Think about this: After a Pharisee sees firsthand how Jesus has dismantled the deceptive arguments of the Sadducees, who believe there is no life after death, he tries to trap Jesus with a question that (he knows) will force Him into a response that will get Him into trouble with religious leaders. He says, "Teacher, which is the most important commandment in the law of Moses?" This Pharisee is referring to the 613 laws of Moses contained in the Torah, which were used to guide the behavior and beliefs of ancient Jews. It's a massive clutter of moral restrictions and imperatives. No matter what "greatest command" Jesus chooses, the Pharisees are ready to attack. But Jesus goes all Marie Kondo on the man's question, decluttering and simplifying with this: "'You must love the Lord your God with all your heart, all your soul, and all your mind.' This is the first and greatest commandment. A second is equally important: 'Love your neighbor as yourself.' The entire law and all the demands of the prophets are based on these two commandments" (Matthew 22:36–40). From 613 complex and competing laws to just two imperatives: Love God. Love others. And the Pharisee doesn't know what to say in response.

This is not a one-time anomaly in how Jesus approached His cluttered and messy "belief environment"—He is always and everywhere distilling what is most important into only those simple things that reflect the love at the core of God's heart, those things that "spark joy."

So how can we follow the decluttering momentum of Jesus and translate it into our physical environment, using insights and ideas borrowed from a feng shui philosophy that (on the surface) has nothing to do with Him?

• **Our consumer culture has produced an epidemic of "too much-ness," so pare down to only those things that hold meaning and value for you.** Do a quick inventory of what is on your walls and surfaces in your living spaces, then experiment by removing some things that (truly) have marginal value to you. Start small and see where this takes you.

• **Buy used or new furniture that is simple, durable, beautiful, and functional.** Look for clean, simple lines, elegant but long-lasting fabrics, and pieces that offer storage flexibility.

• **Surround yourself with possessions and decorations that are tied to personal values and passions.** For example, in my (Rick's) home, we have a quasi-impressionist (and colorful) painting of a road leading to a forested home that is mounted above our fireplace. This reminds me, in a subtle way, of the journey I'm on to my "true home" with Jesus. And in our dining area, I have a stylized print of a jazz master playing his bass; it reminds me of the beauty of improvisational jazz, which is a metaphor for my relationship with Jesus.

• **Find organizing containers that will help you gather needed clutter into a simple space.** Think through how often you use certain items and make the most-used things readily available in your storage system.

• **Reorganize your furniture and belongings to create open spaces and a sense of "flow" in your home.** Closed-in spaces create tension, so work to open up your environment in whatever way you can. When we're unable to move easily around our environment, it produces frustration, and even low-frequency hopelessness. Opening up and decluttering your spaces can give your brain health a boost.

7. **Light Boosters.** In the last few decades, a light-related psychological condition called seasonal affective disorder (SAD) has emerged as a significant driver of depression in those experiencing natural-light deprivation. Simply put, when we aren't exposed to enough natural light (especially during the late fall, winter, and early spring), some

suffer from what's been called "seasonal blues." The name sounds harmless, even quaint. But the depressive impact of light deprivation is no joke. A lack of natural light can kickstart a deep depression.[17] And it's not just the diminished light coming from the sun that is challenging; poor office or home lighting can also fuel the stress and anxiety that make "withdrawals" from your brain health. Light is life—and Jesus made this a huge metaphorical emphasis in His teaching: "I am the light of the world. If you follow me, you won't have to walk in darkness, because you will have the light that leads to life" (John 8:12).

Researchers have found both direct and indirect "light influences" on mood—"impaired vision or inadequate light reception can aggravate depressive symptoms."[18] How? We have three photoreceptors in our eyes, and when one of them is directly exposed to light, it sends a response to the same brain region that affects our emotions. But it's the indirect impact of sleep disruption, brain plasticity, neurotransmission, hormone secretion, and gene expression that clearly impacts mood disorders. Some studies show structural changes to the brain in patients who've experienced severe circadian disruptions—international flight attendants, for example.[19] What can we do to make up for light deprivation, both natural and artificial, in our everyday environments?

• **Get a SAD lamp to supplement your interior lighting.** Because sunlight is sparse during half of the year, we need a "transfusion" of natural light, and a special SAD light can help. Many, many varieties are available online at all price points.

• **Change your home and office lighting.** In a European study funded by the office-supply chain Staples, researchers discovered that four out of ten workers struggle through their daily routines under poor lighting. Almost all of the workers interviewed for the study (80 percent) said that good lighting in their workspace is important to them, and a third (32 percent) said better lighting would make them happier. Some workplaces are paying attention, giving their employees "biodynamic lighting"—an artificial source of light that maps to the variations of daylight and sunlight over the course of the day using a light management system. "Cold" lighting is a kind of stimulant, alerting the brain to wake up and pay attention. But "warm" lighting can function like a comforting blanket—candlelight, in particular, is soothing. Find a way every evening to light at least one candle in your living space. A candle centerpiece on your dining table is a great way to make sure you do this. But you can use candles in your bedroom, bathroom, and kitchen area as well.

• **Walk or bike and don't ride or drive, whenever possible.** We shield ourselves from at least some natural light whenever we're inside a structure or a vehicle or a train. So think about your shorter errands or commitments and consider whether you can walk or bike to them instead. If you make time for exercise every week, consider replacing an indoor workout with an outdoor workout.

• **Rearrange your home or office workspace to move your desk near a window.** If you have a choice between window seating and central seating, always choose the window. And look at your home with a creative eye—determine where you spend most of your day and rearrange what you can to give yourself the most exposure to outdoor light. If you live in an apartment or condo complex, spend part of your workday or down-time on the roof (if it's accessible), balcony (if you have one), or in a nearby park or green space.

• **Expose yourself to short periods of bright light.** Long stretches of bright light are actually stressful and depression-inducing. But short bursts of it (five to fifteen minutes) can actually wake up your senses and your soul.[20] So spend your devotional or reading time sitting directly under a lamp or in direct sunlight. Don't stay too long, though.

8. **Change Anything.** Mark Zuckerberg, Facebook's CEO, has famously worn the same basic gray T-shirt to work every day as leader of one of the most valuable tech companies in the world. When a reporter asked him why he didn't change it up a little, Zuckerberg

said: "I really want to clear my life to make it so that I have to make as few decisions as possible about anything except how to best serve this community. I'm in this really lucky position, where I get to wake up every day and help serve more than a billion people. And I feel like I'm not doing my job if I spend any of my energy on things that are silly or frivolous about my life." Zuckerberg has embraced his sartorial rut, and he's manufactured a plausible-sounding explanation for it. But in general, rutted behaviors like his don't help in our determination to leave psychological ruts behind. A change in our habits or our surroundings can be the jolt we need to make changes in other areas of our life.

In a study that focused on the interplay between habits and intentions, researchers discovered that college students who transferred were the most likely to also change their daily habits. It turns out that "familiar external cues" route us into behavioral ruts, and changing those cues gives us permission to leave our rut.[21] Our familiar patterns goad us into familiar behaviors, and vice versa. For example, if you serve dinner on big plates, people will eat more. If you move the candy bowl out of arm's reach, you'll eat less. If your friend at work moves to a workspace further away from your own, you'll spend less time with that friend. A change in the stimulus can have a big impact on our physical and psychological habits. So:

• **Don't try to discipline your way out of rutted thinking.** *Psychology Today* writer Gregory Ciotti says: "Since we know that discipline is built like a muscle—and can likewise be worn out—environmental changes might be useful in getting ourselves to do difficult tasks regularly."[22] This translates to changing our habits in simple ways. To make sure you get the exercise you need to head off depressive cycles, for example, lay out your workout clothes the night before, or decide to attend a regular class instead of working out on your own (the commitment to the class can nudge you to keep at it). Or, for every "hopeless narrative" you share with your spouse or a friend, decide to share one "hopeful narrative."

Bring more color and beauty into your life by buying and displaying low-cost, long-lasting cut flowers (mums, alstroemerias, carnations, chrysanthemums, orchids, and zinnias are all good choices). Get more sunlight every day by using ten minutes of your lunch break for a short walk. Change a habit, even a small one, to break up the "dam" in your destructive thinking and start the flow of hope.

• **Keep some routines so you can play with others.** It's comforting to have stable, dependable routines in our life—they act like trustworthy friends. So keep the routines that (to use Marie Kondo's phrase again) "spark joy" and make a change in those that are neutral. Do you travel the same route to work or walk your dog in the same pattern every day? Try a new path, just to stimulate your brain and engage your soul in new surroundings. Do you haul out the same Christmas decorations every year? Experiment with something completely different for one year and decide what changes you'll keep going forward. Do you listen to the same radio show or podcast on your commute? Try a random new show and listen for your entire commute. The goal is to reactivate your brain out of rutted ways of thinking—for your own good. The more pliable your brain habits, the more likely you can change the internal patterns that lead to destructive narratives.

• **Join a new community group to expose yourself to new relationships.** Sometimes our relational climate is subtly driving us back into our dark valley, and we're unaware of it. All of us have toxic people in our lives, and it's easy to underestimate their impact on our struggles with depression and suicidality. So make a change in your friendship environment by getting involved in a new group or activity at your church, community center, fitness center, or neighborhood.

Upsetting the Apple Cart

When a rich, earnest, and self-satisfied young man comes to Jesus seeking a gold star for his moral performance, Jesus feels "genuine love" for him. But He's studying this man and spots the cancer of self-righteousness growing in him: if the man remains in his check-all-the-boxes rut, it's going to kill his soul. So Jesus invites this unsuspecting do-gooder into a radical change: "Go and sell all your possessions and give the money to the poor, and you will have treasure in heaven. Then come, follow me" (Mark 10:17–22). The change seems just too big, too radical, too costly. And the man walks away sad. But Jesus is trying to leverage an internal change by inviting him into an external change—because He loves him and doesn't want him to implode under the pressure of his religious rule-keeping.

The light is always fighting back against the darkness—a metaphorical truth in our relationship with Jesus, but also a physical truth in our journey out of the valley.

WHAT YOU CAN DO IF . . .

You're the One Who's Struggling	You Care for Someone Who's Struggling
• Try a new shampoo or soap based on aroma alone. Buy an inexpensive diffuser and experiment with essential oils until you find one you really like.	• Surprise your friend or loved one with fresh-cut flowers as often as possible.
• Painting an interior space is one of the easiest, cheapest ways to radically transform your environment. Consider "nature colors" as a foundational or complementary color.	• If the person you're caring for is in your home, consider your color scheme and the lighting you currently have and make one change that reflects brain-healthy colors.

• Get your hearing checked and get help if you need it, listen to an instrumental channel on Spotify or another music service, and visit fcfrmd.com and search for "Good Vibrations" for more ideas.	• Turn off the TV in your home, if it's often used as "background noise," and turn on instrumental music instead.
• Get an air purifier (you'll find many options online at every price level) and use it in your main living area.	• Invite your friend or loved one on "fresh-air" outings— parks, hiking trails, beaches, and anywhere not directly impacted by car and industrial pollutants.
• You've heard this many times: drink plenty of liquids during the day, dress in lightweight and light-colored clothing, and stay out of the heat of the day.	• When you buy gifts of clothing for your friend or loved one, look for lightweight or light-colored garments.
• Brainstorm new ways to arrange the furniture in your home to maximize feng shui and declutter your living spaces.	• If your friend or loved one has a cluttered living space, offer to help by relating your own experiences of decluttering (and giving away things to charities that can use what you have), then offer to help do the same for your friend.
• Get SAD lamps for your interior spaces and make sure your home is well-lit with amber-colored light, if possible.	• Give your friend or loved one a decorative candle, and when you meet together, always choose the place closest to an outside window.

CHAPTER 12

LOOKING OUT INSTEAD OF IN

Why Outward-Focused Habits of Generosity and Friendship-Building Can Keep Us from Descending into Rutted Patterns of Destruction

When Matthew Warren was twelve, his descent into suicidal ideation set in. His parents, Rick and Kay Warren—well-known around the world as founding pastors of Saddleback Community Church in Orange County, California—knew early on that Matthew was different from his older siblings. As a child he was diagnosed with panic disorder, attention-deficit/hyperactivity disorder, and early-onset bipolar disorder. For Kay, Matthew's struggles touched on an ache she'd known well her whole life: "I don't really remember a time when I didn't feel the weight of the world on my shoulders, even when I was a little girl. As a teenager I struggled with depression, but I never heard anybody use that word. I just knew that there were times when I didn't want to talk to my family. I lost interest in school and just had a sadness about me."[1]

As Matthew grew into young adulthood, even with the intervening help of a family that sometimes orbited around his mental-health issues, his depression grew, says Kay, into "an overwhelming desire to be out of pain." He was in and out of hospitals for treatment. But on

April 5, 2013, while away from the protective reach of his parents, Matthew bought a gun on the black market and took his own life. The news of his death reverberated through a Christian community that had generally compartmentalized mental health challenges as failures of faith. As a result, the Warrens were quickly thrust into a leadership role as mental-health advocates.

Meanwhile, Kay was coming to grips with the depth of Matthew's struggles while reentering an exploration of her own battle with depression. And she was rethinking the church's role in helping others who struggle with the same demons that took her son's life. "Unfortunately," she says, "Christianity has tended to color mental illness negatively. It's seen as either demonization or spiritual weakness— 'Well, you can pray it away.' What I've learned…is that we're whole— we are material and immaterial. What happens in one part of our self is going to affect the rest of our self. Conversely, when there's healing and health in one part of us, it also then affects positively the rest of who we are. The church has a very vital role in all of this—nobody is better qualified to speak to the humanity of the person, to the dignity of the person, than the church. It was one of the first institutions to build mental hospitals. So we've had kind of a mixed history, both caring for people who are vulnerable and at the same time pushing them away. So we can come back to that place of embracing and caring for people."[2]

Remarkably, as Kay entered more deeply into her own story, she discovered that her lifelong relationship with depression had given her some powerful tools for reaching and helping others. "There is a definite disadvantage to being wired the way I am," she says, "there's no doubt about that. But depression for me is not debilitating—it's been more of a nagging headache than a migraine. And that nagging headache of depression has made me extremely compassionate. It's enabled me to enter into the pain and the sorrow and the suffering that other people feel in ways that I probably wouldn't be able to access if I didn't also live with depression. I think I'm a better minister because I live with depression. And I'm not really interested in getting rid of it, because I would lose some of the deep compassion that I operate out of."³

Under the guiding influence of a beauty-out-of-ugly Jesus, Kay Warren is walking her journey through the Valley of the Shadow of Death with a determination to look out toward others—to take what was "intended to harm" and give it to God, who uses it to extend the redemptive reach of His heart, "intend[ing] it all for good" (Genesis 50:20). She founded the Hope for Mental Health Initiative through Saddleback as a way to support those struggling with suicidal ideation (and their families) and train ministry people to launch or grow their own outreach strategies. The Initiative also has produced books, training resources, and a video-based starter kit for churches (kaywarren. com/mentalhealthkit). And Kay now serves as a board member with the National Action Alliance for Suicide Prevention. The outward momentum of her life, fueled by lament and courageous self-awareness, is helping bring freedom to captives. This lifestyle of outward-looking habits can help others who are living under the shadow of depression and suicidal ideation.

I (Daniel) often work with professionals who care for others (ministers, clinicians, caretakers, animal lovers, and service providers) and creatives (artists, musicians, and entrepreneurs). In this sub-population of "outward-focused" givers, I find patterns of brain activity that increase the ability to "feel"—often to a much greater depth than others. This developed strength empowers the givers to care more than others, to be intolerant of "wrongs" and seek to fix them, and to have an outsize impact on their environment. I call it their superpower.

But like every superhero, their power is often linked to their vulnerability. When that superpower of caring is combined with their innate gifts, education, opportunity, and positive feedback, they can thrive. Unfortunately, because they feel so deeply for others, they will also feel the pain and disappointment of life more acutely. Repeated traumas, disappointments, limited opportunities, and limited positive feedback can drain their strength. And a disempowered brain with a "feeling" superpower can be debilitating.

The strategies in this book are developed to uplift and harness this superpower—to help build a bulwark against the downward pull of depression and suicidality. Our menu of possibilities will not eradicate pain from your life, but these habits can reduce it, bring meaning to it, and invite Jesus to redeem it. You have something others desperately need—and it's important to remember that.

A Hermeneutic of Generosity

Dr. Paul Farmer, the legendary infectious disease expert, Harvard professor, and globe-trotting activist for public-health innovation, is a determined advocate for what he calls the "H of G." It's short for "hermeneutic of generosity"—meaning he's operating from a foundation that assumes the best in others and is determined to reach out to help others as a default setting in life.[4] Put another way, Farmer has intentionally decided to live a lifestyle that "gives what he has to give" in service to others. This is not only a guaranteed path to having a good impact in life, but also a powerful mental-health therapy. In an online survey of more than four thousand adults in the United Kingdom, two-thirds (63 percent) of the respondents said "being kind to others has a positive impact on their mental health." And in a systematic review of existing research on the link between outward-looking behaviors and psychological health, a team of academics found that kindness toward others had a clear correlation with mental well-being.[5]

It's important to remember that those who are living under the shadow of depression are more likely to:

- Focus blame on themselves when something goes wrong
- Assume that other people don't like them
- Experience a general sense of dislike for themselves
- Interpret their actions in the worst possible light
- Fixate on the mistakes they've made[6]

These internal beliefs act like termites, eating away at self-esteem and propelling the person deeper into the shadows. It makes sense, then, that anything that is effective in driving away the termites will help us find our footing and resist the magnetic pull toward the darkness.

When researchers explored strategies for undergirding self-worth, they compared two approaches—one inward-looking and one outward-looking. The first approach focused on giving people self-image goals—"obtaining status or approval and avoiding vulnerability during social interactions." They were asked to promote their positive qualities to others and avoid revealing their weaknesses. The second approach focused on "compassionate goals," or "striving to help others and avoiding selfish behavior." They were asked to explore "making a positive difference in someone else's life." The result, according to the study's authors, was that "participants reported higher conflict and symptoms on days that they most pursued self image goals, but noted higher perceived support and lower symptoms when pursuing compassionate goals."[7]

When we redirect our energy and attention away from our internal maelstroms and toward others' needs, the pull toward depression is slowed or even neutralized. We tend to set aside our internal chaos when our hands are full trying to help others. In that light, here are two broad strategies for making outward-focused habits integral to your lifestyle:

1. **Relational Generosity.** Simply put, be proactively enthusiastic about others' good news and proactively compassionate toward their bad news. When others make a mistake or have a moral failure, a reaction that focuses on our universally broken humanity instead of feeding their inherent shame can invite them to repent and forgive themselves and, in turn, bolster your own appreciation for grace. Focus on constructive rather than destructive responses to others— look for the lurking beauty in them, even when the ugly seems dominant. When we spot and highlight the image of God in others, we open ourselves to embracing the image of God in ourselves. Jesus reminds us: "God blesses those who are merciful, for they will be shown mercy" (Matthew 5:7).

During the COVID-19 pandemic, scores of people found creative ways to care for their neighbors, from doing their grocery shopping to leaving meals on their doorstep to sending them food-delivery gift cards. Though these ideas were born out of a crisis, they are not crisis-specific. "Going the extra mile" for others can simply be our new norm. Actor John Krasinski's brief online show *Some Good News* highlighted a vast array of others-focused acts of relational generosity— go to YouTube.com and search for "Some Good News" to sample the ideas. The Apostle Paul drilled down into the mechanics of relational generosity with this list of Kingdom-of-God habits, all of them embedded in the "native culture" of the Trinity:

- Love is patient and kind.
- Love is not jealous or boastful or proud or rude.
- It does not demand its own way.
- It is not irritable, and it keeps no record of being wronged.
- It does not rejoice about injustice but rejoices whenever the truth wins out.

- Love never gives up, never loses faith, is always hopeful, and endures through every circumstance (1 Corinthians 13:4–7).

These descriptions seem daunting because they are. Most of us struggle to respond to others this way in the best of times—and a "disciplined approach" is not a possible path when you're struggling just to get out of bed in the morning. But Paul is describing the fruits of love, not the disciplines required to express it. Relational generosity—the kind that is patient and humble and forgiving and rejoicing and persevering—is the "produce" of the Spirit of Jesus in us. We trust in His heart to move toward others in this way, not in our own discipline or effort. Put another way, we give way to the heart of Jesus in us by inviting Him to relate generously toward others through us. We trust Him, over and over and over, to respond to others with a generosity that redirects our gaze outward.

2. Giving from Our Good Treasure. A heart captured by the love of God wants to give. When we deepen our relationship with Jesus, we get infected by His heart, and He's always spending the treasure of what He has to give to others. But again, it seems hard to think of giving to others when we're slogging through the Valley of the Shadow of Death and feel like we have nothing left in our tank. Writer Daphne Merkin describes what it's like to be caught in the grip of suicidality:

> When I was awake (the few hours that I was), I felt a kind of lethal fatigue, as if I were swimming through tar. Phone messages went unanswered, email unread. In my inert but agitated state I could no longer concentrate long enough to read—not so much as a newspaper headline—and the idea of writing was as foreign to me as downhill racing.[8]

This feeling of emptiness and need is like a veil covering the portal to our way out of the valley. But if we will walk through the veil and look for ways to give, we can find strength and energy bubbling up inside.

Therese Borchard, founder of Project Beyond Blue, an online community for people who struggle with chronic depression and anxiety, recalls what psychiatrist Dr. Karl Menninger said when he was asked: "What would you advise a person to do, if that person felt a nervous breakdown coming on?" Menninger, she says, upended the expected response ("Go see a psychiatrist") with this: "Leave your house, find someone in need, and do something to help that person."[9] Remember that scene in *It's a Wonderful Life*, when George Bailey is about to jump off a bridge into the icy water below until he witnesses another man beat him to it (the innocently shrewd angel Clarence)? Alarmed, George strips off his jacket and dives into the water to save the drowning man. Once inside the bridge toll–keeper's warming hut, Clarence explains his lifesaving strategy:

> Toll-Keeper: How'd you happen to fall in?
> Clarence: I didn't fall in. I jumped in to save George.
> (George looks up, surprised)
> George: You what? To save me?
> Clarence: Well, I did, didn't I? You didn't go through with it, did you?
> George: Go through with what?
> Clarence: Suicide. (George and the toll-keeper react to this)
> Toll-Keeper: It's against the law to commit suicide around here.
> Clarence: Yeah, it's against the law where I come from, too.
> Toll-Keeper: Where do you come from? (He leans forward to spit, but is stopped by Clarence's next statement)

Clarence: Heaven. (to George) I had to act quickly; that's why I jumped in. I knew if I were drowning you'd try to save me. And you see, you did, and that's how I saved you.[10]

The psychological label for what George Bailey does in this scene is called a "positive activity intervention." The drive to help others in need generates a burst of depression-fighting energy. Sonja Lyubomirsky, a psychology professor at the University of California, has studied the phenomenon: "They seem really trivial [acts of giving to others]. They seem like, what's the big deal, you feel good for ten minutes. But for a depressed person, they aren't trivial at all. Depressed individuals need to increase positive emotions in their life, even a minute here and there."[11] In short, if you're struggling with depression, you can find help for yourself by helping others. And that means putting yourself in a stream of giving, where opportunities to give flow toward you, without sapping your "discipline reserves." Ideas include:

• **Find a cause or an outreach or a "people group" that captures your heart, then volunteer for a local community organization that serves that passion.** Get close to people in need, and their need will draw out your strength. You can find organizations that serve refugees, the elderly, people with special needs, the poor, veterans, at-risk teenagers, and abuse survivors by searching online or posting your request on a neighborhood online community board such as Nextdoor (nextdoor.com).

• **Give from your maturity and expertise as a mentor.** When I (Rick) was just out of college, I had a friend who invited me to help lead a chapel service for incarcerated teenagers. I'd never been inside a jail facility before, and chapel included two armed guards standing at the back of the room. But I loved giving to those tough-looking kids who, inside, were scared and needy and searching for hope. After six months or so, I was allowed to meet with kids one-on-one in their cells for conversation and "counseling." It was through this experience that my love for inviting others into a more intimate relationship with Jesus surfaced and blossomed. If you have struggled with depression, you already have what so many others need—compassion born out of life experience. Plug "Mentoring in (your state)" in a search engine and you'll find plenty of leads. Or ask someone you know who's already mentoring about their experience.

• **Contact a local school to find volunteer opportunities.** Schools have all kinds of options for helping administrators, students, and coaches. Most are understaffed in their counseling offices and could use people who can help students apply for college scholarships or navigate their class schedules. Some are looking for help coaching sports teams (including special-needs activities like Unified Basketball) or leading extracurricular clubs such as Future Business Leaders of America, Key Club, National Honor Society, and others. If you have a special interest (chess, auto mechanics, Ultimate Frisbee, computer coding, or public speaking, for example), maybe you can start something that isn't currently offered at a school. Grade schools are always looking for classroom or playground helpers and readers.

• **Join friends and neighbors in a community project.** Volunteer at a community garden, join a community clean-up crew, or offer your skills for after-school tutoring. If your neighborhood has a homeowner association, look into the available volunteer roles. Some neighborhoods plan special seasonal gatherings for children (Halloween, Christmas, summer-fun activities) and are always looking for helpers.

• **Start or join a book or film club.** Many neighborhoods have an ongoing multi-generational gathering for book or film lovers. This is a great way to expand your community and find vigorous, challenging conversation. And these clubs are like breeding grounds for new friendships. If in-person participation is not possible, check out one of the many online clubs that popped up during the COVID-19 pandemic and have continued.

• **Offer to teach (or ask to learn) a skill.** If you play an instrument, cook or bake, act or perform musical theater, or have fitness instruction in your background, there are others in your community who would love to learn what you know. For example, if you have been practicing aerobics for years, maybe it's time to share what you've learned with others who really need the physical and social benefits of a class—just post a time and place for a regular outdoor meet-up.

• **Audition for community theater or performance groups.** If you love acting or singing or playing an instrument, search online for local performing groups that are accepting new members or posting auditions.

• **Give back to first responders and military personnel.** Bring food and drink to the staff of an emergency room or intensive care unit. Buy a box of greeting cards and write notes to military personnel, thanking them for their sacrifice and their service. Visit a fire or police station and bring a special treat they can share or a vase of flowers they can display.

• **Upend the impact of social media by using it to bless others.** Social media has become a pit of negativity, and it can magnify feelings of inadequacy, FOMO (fear of missing out), isolation, depression, anxiety, and self-absorption. That last one—self-absorption—is an insidious byproduct of the medium. The gravitational pull of social media is turning our attention inward, not outward. So instead of simply getting off your social media platforms, decide that you will be a "blessing missionary" in a challenging mission field. Post only those updates that are intended to lift others up, not pull them down. And use social media as your own personal playground for "loving your enemies, and praying for those who persecute you" (Matthew 5:44).

The Lesson of James and John

When the mother of James and John approaches Jesus with a "proposition" (Matthew 20:20–28), it's as if she's following the template for a reality show. An over-functioning Jewish mother whose sons are grown men tries to grease the skids for their "career success" by convincing Jesus to "promote" them—and she does this right in front of the other disciples. "In your Kingdom," she says, "please let my two sons sit in places of honor next to you, one on your right and the other on your left." The seat to the right of a king is designated for a person of "equal dignity and authority,"[12] and the seat to the left is nearly as important.

But Jesus upends this honor grab with: "You don't know what you are asking! Are you able to drink from the bitter cup of suffering I am about to drink?" He follows the brothers' ignorant and arrogant response with a treatise on what a life of honor is all about: "You know that the rulers in this world lord it over their people, and officials flaunt their authority over those under them. But among you it will be different. Whoever wants to be a leader among you must be your servant, and whoever wants to be first among you must become your slave. For even the Son of Man came not to be served but to serve others and to give his life as a ransom for many."

Service is the only accepted currency in the Kingdom of God—and for good reason. Serving others not only invests life in them, but also gives us access to the source of that life in ourselves in order to give it. That means the "living water" Jesus has promised us flows through our own soul on its way to splashing onto others. An outward-looking lifestyle taps into a well of life that refreshes and renews and redeems. And the science proves it.

WHAT YOU CAN DO IF ...

You're the One Who's Struggling	You Care for Someone Who's Struggling
• Proactively, intentionally look for the beauty in others, not the (sometimes more obvious) ugly.	• With your friend or loved one, brainstorm ways to express relational generosity with people in your neighborhood or community, then try one of your ideas together.
• "Leave your house, find someone in need, and do something to help that person."	• Together with your friend or loved one, go where needy people congregate—serve in the Stephen Ministry at your church (https://www. stephenministries.org/default.cfm), or the homeless shelter in your community, or at a special-needs outreach, or as tutors at a local school or community center, or at a hospital's welcome center.
• On social media look for ways to post and highlight ways people are modeling life-giving behaviors and lifestyles.	• Every week post on social media something intended to bless or honor or celebrate your friend or loved one.

FIRST THINGS LAST

We end this book by returning to a "first thing"—depression and suicidality are both a hardware and software challenge. Part Two is an extended expedition into ideas and strategies that work to "debug" our software or psychology. But the wide menu of possibilities we've served up simply won't help if an existing hardware bug that circumvents the impact of those ideas and strategies remains. It makes sense: Your computer problems won't be solved with a software upgrade if you have a problem with your hard drive. When that happens, we need professional help to open up the interior of the computer (our biology) and pinpoint the problem. Once that bug is addressed, the software upgrades (the psychological practices and habits in Part Two) can deliver their full impact. We need traction to escape a mental-health pothole, and that requires both a well-functioning engine and a well-functioning transmission.

In one comparison study, just 16 percent of severely depressed psychotherapy patients experienced a positive outcome; the "software debugging" help they received had very limited impact. But nearly all those patients (83 percent) who received both psychotherapy and pharmacotherapy (biology-related help) experienced a positive outcome.[1] In my (Daniel's) work in the clinic, I have seen how genetic vulnerability (or the patient's family psychiatric or trauma history) combines with temperament, negative life experiences, and a toxic thought life to create severe symptoms. However, those who struggle the most are the ones who have compromised brains (injury, toxicity, infections, and genetic risk factors). These struggling people can only improve after our team has diligently addressed their hardware-based factors.

So the path out of the Valley of the Shadow of Death starts with the hardware interventions we've spotlighted in Part One of this book. Seek professional help if you personally struggle with depression or suicidal thinking. If possible, request a SPECT scan of your brain and follow-up consultations to determine the best game plan for hardware interventions (go to amenclinics.com for more information).

And one last encouragement: When Paul writes to the young church in Corinth, he feels compelled to remind the followers of Jesus in this multi-ethnic, multi-faith, cosmopolitan port city about another kind of "first thing" that will impact every aspect of their lives. He writes: "I did not come with superiority of speech or of wisdom, proclaiming to you the testimony of God. For I determined to know nothing among you except Jesus Christ, and Him crucified" (1 Corinthians 2:2 NASB). In a "first things first" lifestyle, knowing and loving Jesus is the gate to whole-person health. He has come not just to redeem us, but to restore us into wholeness.

ACKNOWLEDGMENTS

From Rick:

This labor of love is really an Easter story—a journey from death to life. After years on the sidelines of an epidemic of suicide and depression in my community, I was disillusioned and frustrated with the typical responses surrounding every tragedy. I have a conviction that Jesus has come not merely to offer us a bridge to salvation, but to restore us to Kingdom-of-God wholeness. And so, I began the journey that led to this book by exploring the interplay between whole-person health and wholehearted discipleship. But I had no "credentials" and no formal training as a mental health professional, so the vision for this work died on the vine. Twice. And then my agent, Greg Johnson, called me out of the blue and asked if I might be interested in a sort of "blind date" phone conversation with Dr. Daniel Emina, the associate medical director of the Amen Clinics. The publishers at Salem Books were looking to pair Daniel with a writing partner who could embrace a mash-up of scientific best-practices related to depression and suicide, filtered through the life and teaching of Jesus. It was an extraordinary resurrection—one that has altered the trajectory of my life, chiefly because that first phone call with Daniel turned into a partnership and then a friendship.

I have learned so much from Daniel that it would be hard to contain all of it in this short space. More than anything, I've deeply appreciated his humble, childlike openness to our intentional conversation around depression and suicide and his firm convictions that are born out of research, practice, and a deep love for God. Thank you, Daniel—this project is really a miracle in my life.

And thank you also to these friends and collaborators and family members who helped fuel this work in me...

- My wife, Bev, who's been (typically) direct and vulnerable and passionate in her input into this journey
- My two girls, Lucy and Emma, who have enriched my life so deeply and opened me up to my own soul
- Chris Bruno, LPC, the much-respected founder of Restoration Counseling Center, who first agreed to walk this writing path with me until our early version of this book hit a dead end
- Greg Johnson, for believing in me through thick and thin and thin again
- The monks at St. Benedict's Monastery near Snowmass, Colorado, for providing me with the most beautiful, still, sacred space to write this book and many others
- Karla Dial, the editorial director at Salem Books and the hands-on editor of this book—her work was smart and surgical and savvy and impassioned, and all deeply appreciated
- Tim Peterson, the publisher at Salem Books, for your advocacy and your vulnerability

From Daniel:

Thank you to my God, for all Glory is His.

Thank you to my mother, who inspires me.

Thank you to my wife, who believes in me.

Thank you to my daughter, who motivates me.

Thank you to my family and friends, who have loved me.

Thank you to my teachers, professors, attendings, and colleagues, who have taught me.

Thank you to Dr. Daniel Amen and the Amen Clinics for granting me a platform to follow God's call on my life.

Thank you to Greg Johnson, Karla Dial, Tim Peterson, and Salem Books for helping Rick and me bring this message to the masses.

And lastly, thank you to Rick for his friendship, skill, vision, and willingness to heed God's direction over and over in this project. This book only happened because he was obedient to God's call on his life. It has been a privilege to do this work together.

HELP & RESOURCES

Crisis Resources

A psychiatric crisis—that is, a situation in which you are a danger to yourself or others as a consequence of mental illness—is no different from a medical crisis. It's appropriate to call 911 or go directly to a hospital emergency room. Emergency medical technicians and 911 operators, as well as police and firefighters, are trained to handle such issues, and they may be your best and fastest resources in the face of an immediate need.

Many specialty hotlines are also available where counselors are trained to deal with specific needs. Most of these have both phone and online chat versions available. These resources are free and available twenty-four hours a day. Some specific recommendations include:

- National Suicide Prevention Lifeline
  1-800-273-8255
  www.suicidepreventionlifeline.org

- National Council on Alcoholism and Drug Dependence Hopeline
  1-800-622-2255
  www.ncaad.org

- National Domestic Violence/Child Abuse/Sexual Abuse Helpline
  1-800-799-7233
  http://www.thehotline.org/help

- Veterans Crisis Line
  1-800-273-8255 ext. 1
  VeteransCrisisLine.net

- National Center for Posttraumatic Stress Disorder
  1-802-296-6300
  http://www.ptsd.va.gov/public/where-to-get-help.asp

- RAINN National Sexual Assault Hotline
  1-800-656-HOPE (4673)
  online.rainn.org

- SAMHSA Disaster Distress National Helpline
  1-800-662-HELP (4357)
  http://disasterdistress.samhsa.gov

- National Youth Crisis Hotline
  1-800-442-HOPE (4673)
  www.hopeline.com

- Compassionate Friends (for parents enduring the loss of a child)
  1-630-990-0010
  www.compassionatefriends.org

- Judi's House (for children dealing with the loss of a parent)
  1-720-941-0331
  www.judishouse.org

- The Alzheimer's Association
  1-800-272-3900

Online Therapy Worksheets

- Psychology Tools: http://psychology.tools/download-therapy-worksheets.html

Internet Resources

- American Pain Society: http://www.americanpainsociety.org
- American Psychological Association: http://www.apa.org/helpcenter/index.aspx.
- Association for Behavioral and Cognitive Therapies: http://www.abct.org/home
- Computer-Based Training for Cognitive Behavioral Therapy (CBT4CBT): http://www.cbt4cbt.com
- The Drinker's Checkup: http://www.drinkerscheckup.com
- Smokefree.gov: http://smokefree.gov
- Substance Abuse and Mental Health Services Administration (SAMHSA): http://www.samhsa.gov/sbirt
- Therapeutic Education System (TES): http://sudtech.org/about
- *Treatments That Work* (Oxford University Press): http://global.oup.com/us/companion.websites/umbrella/treatments

SELF-ASSESSMENTS RECOMMENDED BY AMEN CLINICS

The screeners below are not meant to be diagnostic, but they can be helpful in clarifying what symptoms you are experiencing as an encouragement to seek the support you need.

General Screeners

- https://brainhealthassessment.com (general brain and mental health)
- https://www.helpyourselfhelpothers.org (general screener covering a wide range of symptoms)
- https://psychology-tools.com (repository of screening scales)

ADHD

- https://psychology-tools.com/test/
  adult-adhd-self-report-scale
- https://www.additudemag.com/
  adhd-symptoms-test-adults/
- https://nyulangone.org/files/psych_adhd_checklist_0.
  pdf

Alcohol and Drug Use—CAGE-AID

- https://psychology-tools.com/test/
  cage-alcohol-questionnaire
- https://www.mdcalc.com/cage-questions-alcohol-use
- https://www.hopkinsmedicine.org/johns_hopkins_
  healthcare/downloads/all_plans/CAGE%20Sub-
  stance%20Screening%20Tool.pdf

Anxiety—GAD7

- https://psychology-tools.com/test/gad-7
- https://www.mdcalc.com/gad-7-general-anxiety-disor
  der-7
- https://patient.info/doctor/
  generalised-anxiety-disorder-assessment-gad-7
- https://adaa.org/sites/default/files/
  GAD-7_Anxiety-updated_0.pdf

Automatic Thoughts Questionnaire (ATQ)

The ATQ is a thirty-item instrument that assesses negative thoughts that are associated with depression among adults. It is helpful for identifying automatic negative thoughts, which is the first step in challenging these thoughts: https://hhs.texas.gov/sites/default/files/documents/doing-business-with-hhs/provider-portal/behavioral-health-provider/cognitive-behavioral-therapy-resources/automatic-thoughts-questionnaire.pdf.

Bipolar Disorder YMRS

- https://psychology-tools.com/test/
  young-mania-rating-scale

Depression—PHQ9

- https://psychology-tools.com/test/phq-9
- https://www.mdcalc.com/
  phq-9-patient-health-questionnaire-9
- https://patient.info/doctor/
  patient-health-questionnaire-phq-9
- http://med.stanford.edu/fastlab/research/imapp/msrs/_
  jcr_content/main/accordion/accordion_content3/
  download_256324296/file.res/PHQ9%20id%20
  date%2008.03.pdf

The Dysfunctional Attitude Scale (DAS)

The DAS is a forty-item instrument that is designed to identify and measure cognitive distortions, particularly distortions that may relate to or cause depression. The items contained on the DAS are based on Aaron T. Beck's cognitive therapy model and present seven major value systems: approval, love, achievement, perfectionism, entitlement, omnipotence, and autonomy. This test is helpful for identifying your psychological strengths and emotional vulnerabilities: https://www.themathersclinic.com/wp-content/uploads/2018/pdfs/Mathers-Clinic-Dysfunctional-Attitude-Scale.pdf.

Obsessive Compulsive Inventory— Revised (OCI-R)

- https://psychology-tools.com/test/obsessive-compulsive-inventory-revised

Post-Traumatic Stress Disorder—PC-PTSD-5

- https://psychology-tools.com/test/pc-ptsd-5
- https://www.ptsd.va.gov/professional/assessment/documents/pc-ptsd5-screen.pdf

Helpful Worksheets

- https://positivepsychology.com/
  challenging-automatic-thoughts-positive-thoughts-
  worksheets/

How to Develop an Organizing Principle

Step 1: Take an inventory of your traumas, schemas, cognitive distortions, past successes, core values/talents, contributions to others, short- and long-term goals, and Scripture or quotes that have consistently resonated with you. Review this with a trusted mentor or spiritual advisor, being mindful of hidden distortions or maladaptive assumptions.

Step 2: Fill in the blanks for the below questions based on the inventory you have generated.

Who am I in Christ: _____ (from Scripture and trusted spiritual advisors).

God's call for me in this world: _____ (how I am living out my values or using my talents to bless others; from Scripture and trusted spiritual advisors).

How I respond to challenges: _____ (reframe past maladaptive schemas; being mindful of your most used cognitive distortions; what Scripture has to say).

Areas in my life that I have control of: _____ (areas I am called to agency while still giving ultimate control to God for things in and out of my control).

How can God use my personal pain for His Glory and my redemption: _____ (from Scripture and trusted spiritual advisors).

Frequent lies I tell myself and truths I need to nurture: _____ (lies to watch out for, and quick refutation from Scripture and your learnings).

Step 3: Revisit weekly how you are living by your OP. Gauge quarterly how well your OP speaks to your current challenges and decisions—look for opportunities to refine it. Consider yearly updates to your OP based on your lessons from the prior year and goals for the new year.

NOTES

Foreword

1. K. Willeumier, D. V. Taylor, and D. G. Amen, "Decreased Cerebral Blood Flow in the Limbic and Prefrontal Cortex Using SPECT Imaging in a Cohort of Completed Suicides," *Translational Psychiatry* 1, no. 8 (August 9, 2011): e28, https://doi.org/10.1038/tp.2011.28.
2. D. G. Amen, J. R. Prunella, J. H. Fallon, B. Amen, and C. Hanks, "A Comparative Analysis of Completed Suicide Using High Resolution Brain SPECT Imaging," *Journal of Neuropsychiatry and Clinical Neurosciences* 21, no. 4 (2009): 430–9, doi: 10.1176/jnp.2009.21.4.430.
3. Jordana Cepelewicz, "A Single Concussion May Triple the Long-Term Risk of Suicide," *Scientific American*, February 8, 2016, https://www.scientificameri can.com/article/a-single-concussion-may-triple-the-long-term-risk-of-suicide1/ ?utm_content=bufferb98ff&utm_medium=social&utm_source=linkedin.com &utm_campaign=buffer.

Introduction

1. Lyrics to "Stuck in a Moment That You Can't Get Out of" by Paul Hewson, David Evans, Adam Clayton, and Larry Mullen. © Universal Music Publishing Group.
2. Mark É. Czeisler et al., "Mental Health, Substance Use, and Suicidal Ideation during the COVID-19 Pandemic—United States, June 24–30, 2020," *Morbidity and Mortality Weekly Report* 69, no. 32 (August 14, 2020): 1049–57.

3. According to the most current NIH report on major depression, it's "one of the most common mental disorders in the United States."

Part One Preface

1. National Institute of Mental Health, "Suicide," updated April 2019, www.nimh .nih.gov/health/statistics/suicide.shtml.
2. Holly Hedegaard, Sally C. Curtin, and Margaret Warner, "Suicide Mortality in the United States, 1999–2017," National Center for Health Statistics Data Brief No. 330, November 2018, www.cdc.gov/nchs/products/databriefs/db330 .htm.
3. Steven H. Woolf and Heidi Schoomaker, "Life Expectancy and Mortality Rates in the United States, 1959–2017," JAMA Network, November 26, 2019, https:// jamanetwork.com/journals/jama/article-abstract/2756187?guestAccessKey=c 1202c42-e6b9-4c99-a936-0976a270551f&utm_source=For_The_Media&u tm_medium=referral&utm_campaign=ftm_links&utm_content=tfl&utm_te rm=112619.
4. R. C. Kessler et al., "Lifetime Prevalence and Age-of-Onset Distributions of Mental Disorders in the World Health Organization's World Mental Health Survey Initiative," *World Psychiatry* 6, no. 3 (October 2007): 168–76, https:// www.ncbi.nlm .nih.gov/pmc/articles/PMC2174588/; "Learn about Mental Health," Centers for Disease Control and Prevention, January 26, 2018, https:// www.cdc.gov/mentalhealth/learn.

Chapter 1

1. From the 2016 National Survey on Drug Use and Health (NSDUH). The NSDUH study definition of a major depressive episode is based mainly on the fourth edition of the *Diagnostic and Statistical Manual of Mental Disorders (DSM-IV)*.
2. Befrienders Worldwide, "Suicide Statistics," posted on befrienders.org.
3. Leo Tolstoy, *Anna Karenina* (London, United Kingdom: Penguin Classics, 2004), 1.
4. L. L. Fazakas-DeHoog, K. Rnic, and D. Dozois, "A Cognitive Distortions and Deficits Model of Suicide Ideation," *Europe's Journal of Psychology* 13, no. 2 (2017): 178–93, https://doi.org/10.5964/ejop.v13i2.1238.
5. L. Schmaal et al., "Imaging Suicidal Thoughts and Behaviors: A Comprehensive Review of 2 Decades of Neuroimaging Studies," *Mol Psychiatry* 25 (2020): 408–27, https://doi.org/10.1038/s41380-019-0587-x.
6. D. Evans et al., eds., "Defining Youth Suicide," in *Treating and Preventing Adolescent Mental Health Disorders: What We Know and What We Don't*

Know: A Research Agenda for Improving the Mental Health of Our Youth (Oxford, United Kingdom: Oxford University Press, 2005–2008).

7. Madeline Drexler, "Guns & Suicide: The Hidden Toll," *Harvard Public Health*, n.d., https://www.hsph.harvard.edu/magazine/magazine_article/guns-suicide/.

8. "The Rise of Firearm Suicide among Young Americans," Everytown for Gun Safety, September 10, 2020, https://everytownresearch.org/report/the-rise-of-firearm-suicide-among-young-americans/.

9. Ibid.

10. Ibid.

11. From a personal interview with Chris Bruno by Rick Lawrence, January 13, 2020.

12. S. Mathôt and S. Van der Stigchel, "New Light on the Mind's Eye: The Pupillary Light Response as Active Vision," *Current Directions in Psychological Science* 24, no. 5 (October 9, 2015): 374–78.

13. Interview with Chris Bruno.

Chapter 2

1. Casey Franklin, pastor of the Inversion Community in Denver, Colorado. Used with permission. First quoted in Rick Lawrence, *Spiritual Grit* (Loveland, Colorado: Group Publishing, 2018).

2. Vanessa Friedman, "Andy Spade on Kate Spade's Death: 'There Was No Indication and No Warning,'" *New York Times*, June 6, 2018.

3. From a personal interview with Chris Bruno by Rick Lawrence, January 13, 2020.

4. Pamela B. Rutledge, "The Psychological Power of Storytelling," *Psychology Today*, January 16, 2011.

5. Elisabeth Camp, "Personal Identity: The Narrative Self," a Kahn Academy video lesson, https://www.khanacademy.org/partner-content/wi-phi/wiphi-metaphysics-epistemology/wiphi-mind/v/personal-identity-the-narrative-self.

6. L. L. Fazakas-DeHoog, K. Rnic, and D. Dozois, "A Cognitive Distortions and Deficits Model of Suicide Ideation," *Europe's Journal of Psychology* 13, no. 2 (2017): 178–93, https://doi.org/10.5964/ejop.v13i2.1238.

7. Lianne Schmaall et al., "Imaging Suicidal Thoughts and Behaviors: A Comprehensive Review of 2 Decades of Neuroimaging Studies," *Mol Psychiatry* 25 (2020): 408–27, https://doi.org/10.1038/s41380-019-0587-x.

Chapter 3

1. Lindsay Christensen, "The Healing Power of Sunlight for Mold-Induced Illness," ascent2health.com, August 9, 2017.

2. G. A. Jacob, and A. Arntz, "Schema Therapy for Personality Disorders—a Review," *International Journal of Cognitive Therapy* 6, no. 2, (2013): 171–85; Eshkol Rafaeli, David P. Bernstein, and Jeffrey Young, *Schema Therapy* (CBT Distinctive Features Series) (New York: Routledge, 2011); Janet S. Klosko and Jeffrey Young, *Reinventing Your Life: The Breakthrough Program to End Negative Behavior and Feel Great Again* (New York: Dutton, 1993); Jeffrey E. Young, Janet S. Klosko, and Marjorie E. Weishaar, *Schema Therapy: A Practitioner's Guide* (New York: Guilford Press, 2003).

3. From the Schema Therapy Institute of South Africa, www.schematherapysout hafrica.co.za.

4. Amy Dickinson, "Ask Amy," Tribune Content Agency, June 25, 2020.

Chapter 4

1. K. L. Lapane et al., "Religion and Cardiovascular Disease Risk," *Journal of Religion and Health* 36, (June 1997): 155–63.

2. Rick Lawrence, "The Heresy We Love," *GROUP Magazine*, January/February 2013.

3. Kristine Fellizar, "7 Signs There May Be Inflammation in Your Brain," Bustle, September 25, 2018, https://www.bustle.com/p/7-signs-there-may-be-inflam mation-in-your-brain-11910223.

4. Dr. Daniel Amen, *The End of Mental Illness* (Carol Stream, Illinois: Tyndale Momentum Books, 2020), 68–69.

Chapter 5

1. John Kay, *From Obliquity* (London, United Kingdom: Penguin Group, 2010), 71.

2. "Laser Blasts Viruses in Blood," ScienceDaily, September 5, 2007.

3. John MacArthur, *Reckless Faith: When the Church Loses Its Will to Discern* (Wheaton, Illinois: Crossway Books, 1994).

4. John Prine, "Boundless Love," from *The Tree of Forgiveness*, Oh Boy Records, April 13, 2018.

5. Jane McGrath, "How Can Dolphins Disarm Sea Mines?," howstuffworks.com, July 10, 2008, https://animals.howstuffworks.com/mammals/dolphin-disarm -sea-mine.htm.

Chapter 6

1. Jack Wellman, "Where Did Jesus Travel While on Earth?," Patheos.com, December 17, 2015, https://www.patheos.com/blogs/christiancrier/2015/12/17 /where-did-jesus-travel-while-on-earth/.

2. Robby Gallaty, *The Forgotten Jesus* (Grand Rapids, Michigan: Zondervan, 2017), 96–97.

3. Julius Ohrnberger, Eleonora Fichera, and Matt Sutton, "The Relationship between Physical and Mental Health: A Mediation Analysis," *Social Science & Medicine* 195 (December 2017): 42–49.

4. Marc Ashley Harris, "The Relationship between Physical Inactivity and Mental Wellbeing: Findings from a Gamification-Based Community-Wide Physical Activity Intervention," *Health Psychology Open* 5, no. 1 (January–June 2018).

5. "Major Depression: The Impact on Overall Health," Blue Cross/Blue Shield, May 10, 2018, https://www.bcbs.com/the-health-of-america/reports/major-depression-the-impact-overall-health.

6. Eva Oberlea et al., "Screen Time and Extracurricular Activities as Risk and Protective Factors for Mental Health in Adolescence: A Population-Level Study," *Preventive Medicine* 141, no. 106291 (December 2020).

7. J. M. Twenge et al., "Increases in Depressive Symptoms, Suicide-Related Outcomes, and Suicide Rates among U.S. Adolescents after 2010 and Links to Increased New Media Screen Time," *Clinical Psychological Science* 6, no. 1 (2018): 3–17, https://doi.org/10.1177/2167702617723376.

8. Lina Sun, Oingshan Sun, and Jinshun Qi, "Adult Hippocampal Neurogenesis: An Important Target Associated with Antidepressant Effects of Exercise," *Reviews in the Neurosciences* 28, no. 7 (2017): 693–703, https://doi.org/10.15 15/revneuro-2016-0076.

9. "Sleep and Mental Health," Harvard Health Publishing, March 18, 2019.

10. N. M. Simon et al., "Efficacy of Yoga vs Cognitive Behavioral Therapy vs Stress Education for the Treatment of Generalized Anxiety Disorder: A Randomized Clinical Trial," *JAMA Psychiatry* 78, no. 1 (August 12, 2020): 13–20, doi:10 .1001/jamapsychiatry.2020.2496.

11. "Worldwide Survey of Fitness Trends for 2020," American College of Sports Medicine, October 30, 2019.

Chapter 7

1. Agnes E. van den Berg et al., "Green Space as a Buffer between Stressful Life Events and Health," *Social Science & Medicine* 70, no. 8 (April 2010): 1203–10, https://doi.org/10.1016/j.socscimed.2010.01.002.

2. Matthew P. White, Ian Alcock, and Benedict W. Wheeler, "Would You Be Happier Living in a Greener Urban Area? A Fixed-Effects Analysis of Panel Data," *Psychological Science*, April 23, 2013.

3. Diana E. Bowler et al., "A Systematic Review of Evidence for the Added Benefits to Health of Exposure to Natural Environments," *BMC Public Health* 10, no. 456 (2010), https://doi.org/10.1186/1471-2458-10-456.

4. Ephrat Livini, "The Japanese Practice of 'Forest Bathing' Is Scientifically Proven to Be Good for You," World Economic Forum, March 23, 2017, weforum.org.
5. Adam C. Landon, Kyle M. Woosnam, and Gerard T. Kyle, "Psychological Needs Satisfaction and Attachment to Natural Landscapes," *Environment and Behavior*, May 21, 2020.
6. E. Morita et al., "Psychological Effects of Forest Environments on Healthy Adults: Shinrin-Yoku (Forest-Air Bathing, Walking) as a Possible Method of Stress Reduction," *Public Health* 121, no. 1 (2007): 54–63, doi: 10.1016/j.puhe.2006.05.024.
7. Pawel Sokal and Karol Sokal, "The Neuromodulative Role of Earthing," *Med Hypotheses*, National Institutes of Health, November 2011.
8. Richard M. Ryan et al., "Vitalizing Effects of Being Outdoors and in Nature," *Journal of Environmental Psychology* 30, no. 2 (June 2010): 159–68, https://doi.org/10.1016/j.jenvp.2009.10.009.
9. Paul Biegler, "Autonomy, Stress, and Treatment of Depression," *British Medical Journal*, May 10, 2008.
10. George MacKerron and Susana Mourato, "Happiness Is Greater in Natural Environments," *Global Environmental Change* 23, no. 5 (October 2013): 992–1000, https://doi.org/10.1016/j.gloenvcha.2013.03.010.

Chapter 8

1. From an interview with Neil Conan on NPR's *Talk of the Nation*, "Thinking 'Counter Clockwise' to Beat Stress," August 2, 2012.
2. Steve Merritt, "Down to the Wire," *GROUP Magazine*, September/October 2013. Used with permission.
3. From the Wikipedia entry for "Lectio Divina, " https://en.wikipedia.org/wiki/Lectio_Divina.

Chapter 9

1. David Foster Wallace, *Infinite Jest* (New York: Back Bay Books, 2006), 696–97.
2. Gang Wu et al., "Understanding Resilience," *Frontiers in Behavioral Neuroscience*, February 15, 2013, https://doi.org/10.3389/fnbeh.2013.00010.
3. Gabor Mate, *When the Body Says No* (Hoboken, New Jersey: Wiley, 2011), 87.
4. Aubrey Sampson, *Sing a Louder Song* (Colorado Springs, Colorado: NavPress, February 5, 2019), 12.
5. David Brooks, "Introspective or Narcissistic?," *New York Times*, August 7, 2014.
6. Ibid.

7. Joseph Campbell, *The Hero with a Thousand Faces* (Princeton, New Jersey: University Press, 2nd edition, 1968), 23.

8. Chris Bruno, *The Brotherhood Primer* (Fort Collins, Colorado: Restoration Project, 2013), https://s3.amazonaws.com/kajabi-storefronts-production/sites/71213/themes/3670487/downloads/ABZdkySQ3irmJqykVdwv_gkBxxLxGS6d2Lre5XkWL_Brotherhood_Primer_Introduction.pdf.

9. Oswald Chambers, *My Utmost for His Highest* (Grand Rapids, Michigan: Discovery House Publishers, 2012), taken from a daily posting on Utmost.org on January 2, 2013.

10. Fu Zhongwen, *Mastering Yang Style Taijiquan,* trans. Louis Swaim (Berkeley, California: Blue Snake Books, 1996).

11. Alice G. Walton, "Seven Science-Backed Methods to Get You Out of Your Head," *Forbes*, August 19, 2014, https://www.forbes.com/sites/alicegwalton/2014/08/19/7-science-backed-ways-to-get-out-of-your-head/.

Chapter 10

1. From a private conversation with Bill Gaultiere, founder of the ministry Soul Shepherding, recorded in a blog post titled "Dallas Willard's One Word for Jesus," soulshepherding.org, June 11, 2008.

2. Sabine Koch et al., "Effects of Dance Movement Therapy and Dance on Health-Related Psychological Outcomes: A Meta-Analysis," *The Arts in Psychotherapy* 41, no. 1 (February 2014): 46–64, https://doi.org/10.3389/fpsyg.2019.01806.

3. Vicky Karkou et al., "Effectiveness of Dance Movement Therapy in the Treatment of Adults with Depression: A Systematic Review with Meta-Analyses," *Frontiers in Psychology*, May 3, 2019, https://doi.org/10.3389/fpsyg.2019.00936.

4. F. Lyshak-Stelzer et al., "Art Therapy for Adolescents with Posttraumatic Stress Disorder Symptoms: A Pilot Study," *Art Therapy* 24, no. 4 (2007): 163–69. https://doi.org/10.1080/07421656.2007.10129474.

5. David Alan Sandmire et al., "The Influence of Art Making on Anxiety: A Pilot Study," *Art Therapy: Journal of the American Art Therapy Association* 29, no. 2 (June 13, 2012): 68–73, https://doi.org/10.1080/07421656.2012.683748.

6. Elizabeth R. Kimport and Steven J. Robbins, "Efficacy of Creative Clay Work for Reducing Negative Mood: A Randomized Controlled Trial," *Art Therapy* 29, no. 2 (June 2012), http://dx.doi.org/10.1080/07421656.2012.680048.

7. Liz Brewster and Andrew M. Cox, "The Daily Digital Practice as a Form of Self-Care: Using Photography for Everyday Well-Being," *Health Education & Behavior* 23, no. 4 (April 7, 2018), http://dx.doi.org/10.1177/1363459317876 9465.

8. Aneri Pattani, "How Creative Arts Can Change the Way People Deal with Mental Illness," *Philadelphia Inquirer*, November 5, 2018.

9. Laurence Kirkby, "I Have Suicidal Depression—and Board Games Saved My Life," *ARS Technica*, May 14, 2016, https://arstechnica.com/gaming/2016/05 /i-have-suicidal-depression-and-board-games-saved-my-life/.

10. Heather L. Stuckey and Jeremy Nobel, "The Connection between Art, Healing, and Public Health: A Review of Current Literature," *American Journal of Public Health* 100, no. 2 (February 2010): 254–63, doi: 10.2105/AJPH.2008.156497.

11. Ibid.

12. J. M. White, "Effects of Relaxing Music on Cardiac Autonomic Balance and Anxiety after Acute Myocardial Infarction," *American Journal of Critical Care* 8, no. 4 (July 1999): 220–30.

13. Diana Marcum, "Live Music at Fresno's VA Hospital Makes a Big Difference," *Los Angeles Times*, January 16, 2013.

14. Tamlin S. Conner, Colin G. DeYoung, and Paul J. Silvia, "Everyday Creative Activity as a Path to Flourishing," *Journal of Positive Psychology* 13, no. 2 (November 2016): 181–89, http://dx.doi.org/10.1080/17439760.2016.1257049.

15. Danny Lewis, "Feeling Down? Scientists Say Cooking and Baking Could Help You Feel Better," *Smithsonian*, November 29, 2016, https://www.smithso nianmag.com/smart-news/feeling-down-scientists-say-cooking-and-baking -may-help-you-feel-better-180961223/.

Chapter 11

1. Charles W. Schmidt, "Environmental Connections: A Deeper Look into Mental Illness," *Environmental Health Perspectives*, August 2007, A404–A410.

2. V. W. C. Yim et al., "A Review on the Effects of Aromatherapy for Patients with Depressive Symptoms," *Journal of Alternative Complementary Medicine* 15, no. 2 (February 2009): 187–95, https://doi.org/10.1089/acm.2008.0333.

3. Brian Krans, "Aromatherapy for Depression," medically reviewed by Debra Rose Wilson, healthline.com, May 15, 2018, https://www.healthline.com/hea lth/depression/aromatherapy.

4. Lisa Evans, "Six Scents That Can Transform Your Mood and Productivity," *Entrepreneur Magazine*, October 8, 2012, https://www.entrepreneur.com/ar ticle/224575.

5. Samina T. Yousuf Azeemi and S. Mohsin Raza, "A Critical Analysis of Chromotherapy and Its Scientific Evolution," *Evidence–Based Complementary Alternative Medicine* 2, no. 4 (December 2005): 481–88.

6. Marshall McLuhan and Quentin Fiore, *The Medium Is the Massage: An Inventory of Effects* (London, United Kingdom: Penguin Modern Classics, 2008), 84.

7. Azeemi and Raza, "A Critical Analysis of Chromotherapy and Its Scientific Evolution."

8. Resit Canbeyli, "Sensorimotor Modulation of Mood and Depression: In Search of an Optimal Mode of Stimulation," *Frontiers in Human Neuroscience*, July 30, 2013, https://doi.org/10.3389/fnhum.2013.00428.

9. F. Naqvi et al., "Sub-Chronic Exposure to Noise Affects Locomotor Activity and Produces Anxiogenic and Depressive Like Behavior in Rats," *Pharmacological Reports* 64, no. 1 (2012): 64–9, doi: 10.1016/s1734-1140(12)70731-4.

10. Suzanne Boothby, "Does Music Affect Your Mood?," Healthline.com, April 13, 2017, https://www.healthline.com/health-news/mental-listening-to-music -lifts-or-reinforces-mood-051713#:~:text=New%20research%20shows%20t hat%20even,boost%20happiness%20and%20reduce%20anxiety.&text=Re searchers%20have%20pondered%20the%20possible,benefits%20of%20mu sic%20for%20centuries.

11. "Good Vibrations: A Look at American Moods & Music Choices," Family Center for Recovery website (fcfrmd.com), April 11, 2018, https://fcfrmd.com/ good-vibrations/.

12. "How Your Environment Affects Your Mental Health," National Counseling Society, https://nationalcounsellingsociety.org/blog/posts/how-your-environ ment-affects-your-mental-health#:~:text=Environmental%20factors%20wh ich%20affect%20your,of%20their%20associated%20environmental%20tro ubles.

13. Kirsten Weir, "Smog in Our Brains," *American Psychological Association* 43, no. 7 (July/August 2012), https://www.apa.org/monitor/2012/07-08/smog.

14. James T. Mullins and Corey White, "Temperature and Mental Health: Evidence from the Spectrum of Mental Health Outcomes," *Journal of Health Economics* 68 (December 2019), http://ftp.iza.org/dp12603.pdf.

15. Ibid.

16. Michel Lewis et al., "Coffee, Caffeine, and Risk of Completed Suicide: Results from Three Prospective Cohorts of American Adults," *World Journal of Biological Psychiatry* 15, no. 5 (July 2, 2013): 377–86, doi: 10.3109/15622975.2013.795243.

17. Canbeyli, "Sensorimotor Modulation of Mood and Depression."

18. R. C. Espiritu et al., "Low Illumination Experienced by San Diego Adults: Association with Atypical Depressive Symptoms," *Biology of Psychiatry* 35, no. 6 (March 1994): 780–86, https://doi.org/10.1016/0006-3223(94)90007-8.

19. Christine Dearmont, "How Blue Light Affects Mental Health," Mental Health America, n.d., https://mhanational.org/blog/how-blue-light-affects-mental-he alth.

20. Canbeyli, "Sensorimotor Modulation of Mood and Depression."

21. J. A. Ouellette and W. Wood, "Habit and Intention in Everyday Life: The Multiple Processes by Which Past Behavior Predicts Future Behavior," *Psychological Bulletin* 124, no. 1 (1998): 54–74, https://psycnet.apa.org/doi/10 .1037/0033-2909.124.1.54.

22. Gregory Ciotti, "Want to Change Your Habits? Change Your Environment," *Psychology Today*, August 7, 2014, https://www.psychologytoday.com/us/bl og/habits-not-hacks/201408/want-change-your-habits-change-your-environment.

Chapter 12

1. Rick Lawrence, "Kay Warren on Grief, and Facing Mental Illness," youthministry.com, November 16, 2015, https://youthministry.com/kay-war ren-on-grief-and-facing-mental-illness/.
2. Ibid.
3. Ibid.
4. Tracy Kidder, *Mountains beyond Mountains* (New York: Random House Trade Paperbacks, 2009), 215.
5. O. S. Curry et al., "Happy to Help? A Systematic Review and Meta-Analysis of the Effects of Performing Acts of Kindness on the Well-Being of the Actor," *Journal of Experimental Social Psychology* 76 (May 2018): 320–29.
6. Seth J. Gillihan, "How Helping Others Can Relieve Anxiety and Depression," *Psychology Today*, October 10, 2017, https://www.psychologytoday.com/us/bl og/think-act-be/201710/how-helping-others-can-relieve-anxiety-and-depres sion.
7. Daphne Merkin, "A Journey through Darkness," *New York Times Magazine*, May 6, 2009.
8. Thane M. Erickslon et al., "Compassionate and Self-Image Goals as Interpersonal Maintenance Factors in Clinical Depression and Anxiety," *Journal of Clinical Psychology* 74, no. 4 (April 2018): 608–25, doi: 10.1002/jclp.22524.
9. Therese Borchard, "Want to Lessen Your Depression? Help Someone," *Everyday Health*, March 6, 2015.
10. Frances Goodrich et al., *It's a Wonderful Life* (1946).
11. Borchard, "Want to Lessen Your Depression? Help Someone."
12. "Why Does Scripture Emphasize the Right Hand of God?," GotQuestions.org, https://www.gotquestions.org/right-hand-God.html.

Epilogue

1. Glen O. Gabbard, *Psychodynamic Psychiatry in Clinical Practice*, 5th edition (Washington, D.C.: American Psychiatric Publications, 2014), 228.